HOW 2 TRAIN A:

HOW 2 TRAIN A _____

PATRICIA BARLOW-IRICK

August 2015 Edition

MUSTANG CAMP

LARGO CANYON, NM

How 2 Train A _____
Patricia Barlow-Irick
Publisher information : Self published. No part of this book may be reproduced or transmitted in any form without permission in writing from the author.
Copyright information: All rights reserved. Copyright © 2015 by Patricia Barlow-Irick, Largo Canyon School, Blanco, NM 87412
Cataloging information
Barlow-Irick, Patricia
How 2 Train A _____
ISBN-13: 978-1475192940 (CreateSpace-Assigned)
ISBN-10: 1475192940
BISAC: Pets / General
1.Behavior modification. 2. Reinforcement (Psychology) 3. Conditioned response.

Contents

Preface	6
How to Use This Book:	7
What kind of animal is this?	8
It doesn't matter what kind of critter it is: emotions	10
Neurochemistry, OMG!	13
A Few Extra Words about Fear	18
Methods to Eliminate Fear	23
Like a snowflake.	25
The Ethical Trainer	26
Ethical Dilemma	26
Animal Welfare Notes	30
Laws of Behavior: the Core Concepts	34
1. The Scientific Approach to Changing Behavior	34
2. Behavior: Stimulus – Response Relationships	37
3. Learning	45
3.3 Habituation	47
3.4 Respondent Conditioning	49
3.5 Operant Conditioning	54
3.5.6 Antecedents	56
3.5.8 Behaviors	58
3.5.9 Consequences	62
4. Reinforcement: it increases behaviors	68
4.2 Positive Reinforcement	69
4.4 Negative Reinforcement	73
Cowboy Interlude:	76
5. Punishment: decreases behavior	82
6, Scientific Attitude	89
IMO: the Training Session	93
Antecedents to the Session	93
Training Procedures in Action.	109
Trainer Behaviors in My Repertoire.	122
Trainer Consequences	128
Professionalism	132

Preface

From Aardvarks to Zebras, applied behavior science has a rational prescription for creating behavior change.

Animals have been in training since the first animal appeared on earth. The animal had to learn to modify its behavior to adapt to its surroundings, or it didn't survive. Nature is a relentless teacher. Humans come along and start trying to work the rules of behavior to their advantage, but they didn't invent the game. Then some animal trainer gets a slot on late-night television and acts as if he has invented something totally new. Entertaining, yes, but new? Hardly! Scientists busy themselves with making descriptions of the natural world, and at some point they notice that behavior is a natural phenomenon, so turning their spotlight on it, out comes a relatively humble set of observations about how animals learn. That description is part of our cultural heritage. It's a user-friendly set of rules: the Laws of Behavior. You already know them by heart, if not by name, because it is the same set of rules played by every animal on the planet. And you *are* one. Becoming conscious of these rules is enormously useful for an animal trainer.

This book is meant to be a self-instruction course for anyone who wants to learn how to talk like an educated animal trainer. Of course, you can't be one until you've actually trained some animals, but you are going to sound fabulous and you are definitely going to be educated. I want you to learn the vocabulary and use it. Impress your friends, even your FaceBook friends! And while you are at it, you can help correct some of the misinformation people try to use in order to establish credibility! You will be doing them a favor in the long run if they can be truly credible. When you can explain your own style of training accurately and you can critique other styles of training objectively, you are going to be a valuable training resource to your community.

After reviewing the vocabulary (which is shown in **bold** face) and spelling out the rules, I'll give you some ideas how to walk the talk and put the science to use. I want to share the little things that I have learned over the years as an addition to the standard procedures normally used to train animals. Whether you train goldfish or sharks, parrots or condors, rhinos or ponies, cats or dogs, the material in this book applies to your animal. I didn't invent it. It's been there all along, but everyone has been too busy struggling against nature to notice. It's time to go with the flow!

I began writing this book for my mustang training program. I want to thank some great trainers for their influential ideas: Grey Stafford, James O'Heare, Susan Friedman, Steve Martin, Kayce Cover, Joe Layng, Andrew McLean, Bob Bailey, Steve and Shelly Woods, and Alexandra Kurland. These role-models all provided ideas that I have incorporated into my practice. Some personal friends Peggy Hogan and Shawna Corrin-Karrasch have each provided models of horse trainers committed to rational positive methods. The FaceBook group Equine Behavior and Training provided a forum for me to work out some of my explanations.

How to Use This Book:

This book contains a lot of information that you would like to learn (or why would you be reading it?). But you are going to read it and an hour later you are not going to remember much. Sometime after that, you're going to be training an animal and something is going to really stymie you. You're going to wonder how to cope with the training challenge in front of you. Then you are going to think, "Maybe there is something in the How2TrainA book." As you return to peruse the pages, you are going to notice something in the book you didn't before. It will point you to a solution to your problem. Bingo! That is going to happen a bunch of times and gradually, as you need it, you will slowly assimilate every detail. The point of this is that you can't be instantly fluent in the technology. That is what I think Bob Bailey means when he says, "It's simple but it's not easy." Your animals can't be instantly fluent with what they learn either. It takes time and repetition. It takes a large number of successes. It's hard because we have to change ourselves. Let me know how it goes.

Chapter 1

What kind of animal is this?

Study the species of animal you plan to train. Find an **ethogram** (list of typical behaviors) and try to create a catalog of photos of your animal doing species-typical behaviors. If you can't find a prepared ethogram, make your own by developing a list of behaviors and a description of what you actually see when the animal is doing them (try to avoid speculating about why).

Find video clips of this species both in the wild and interacting with humans, and then scrutinize them for typical behaviors. Take notes and become fluent talking about your species behavior. The more you know about your animal's species, the less you are going to have to reinvent the wheel.

Training an animal to perform a species typical behavior on command is a lot easier than training an animal to engage in a completely novel set of actions. Nature has endowed your animal with a rich evolutionary history behind its behavioral repertoire. Use it, if you can. Going against Mother Nature is the hard road.

> **Zebra Threat Behavior Ethogram**
> **Kick threat**
> Presents rump while swishing tail, while facing away, lifts a hind hoof one or more times, then continues turning to face threat.
> **Bite threat**
> Puts ears back against neck, flips lips, exposing teeth, swishing tail with force.

The emotional states of many animals are easily recognizable. Their faces, their eyes, and the ways in which they carry themselves can be used to make strong inferences about what they are feeling. Changes in muscle tone, posture, gait, facial expression, eye size and gaze, vocalizations, and odors (pheromones), singly and together, indicate emotional responses to certain situations. What does this type of animal look like when it is relaxed? What does it look like when it is afraid? What do they do when they panic? Try noticing fine details.

You especially need to know what your animal is likely to do when it is uncomfortable, about to make a run for it, or about to attack you. Imagine that you are training a pig and it is standing with its head low and swinging side to side. What is going to happen next? You could be bitten if you don't figure it out quickly!

Chapter 2

It doesn't matter what kind of critter it is: emotions

Animals don't think in language like we do. When you can't sleep at night and the world is very still, it is a good time to practice not thinking in language to see what that feels like. Things get very sensory-based. Animals can't understand us in language either, even if we whisper. They will take our verbally-given cues as sound signals without a moment of abstract thought. This doesn't mean they are not highly intelligent. Many species can form fairly sophisticated concepts. Some can recognize people from being shown photos but the same species (horses) haven't been shown to learn by watching another horse. We might not be sure of what thought capacities they have, but if we don't expect them to rationally think through their behavior, we will not be disappointed.

Have you ever been chastised for anthropomorphizing? This former breach of propriety has been stepped down quite a bit by new science. Animals do have feelings and even fish feel pain. Scientists can study the physical and chemical changes associated with typical emotional states in humans. Because these same physical changes are found in all mammals in response to situations that would be likely to invoke emotions (such as fear and contentment), we have no basis to say that animals don't feel the same emotions we do. Scientists can produce recognizably similar emotions by stimulation of homologous parts of the brain of species as different as chickens, guinea pigs, and humans. Some researchers suggest that, as in human children, emotions might be even stronger in animals than in adult humans. Our experience with wild horses as downright "Drama-Queens" supports this theory.

To a biologist, emotions are considered as adaptive systems that give animals the ability to avoid harm/punishment or to seek valuable resources/reward. The animal can never stop looking for food, safety, and reproductive opportunities, even following unsuccessful attempts. The impetus of emotions causes the animal to continue investing in the future despite current failures. Emotions clearly have benefits to animals' success at surviving and reproducing. These systems are shared by all mammals, reptiles and birds. The evidence is less clear in amphibians and fish.

Current research provides compelling evidence that most animals likely feel a full range of emotions, including fear, joy, happiness, shame, embarrassment, resentment, jealousy, rage, anger, love, pleasure, compassion, respect, relief, disgust, sadness, despair, and grief. The typical objections to saying animals feel these things are that we have no way to know for sure what they feel. But really.... how can you know for sure that anyone but yourself feels an emotion the way you experience it?

The cognitive theory of emotion holds that the animal reacts to stimuli with an almost automatic, semi-visceral **appraisal** based on prior experience and expectation. If the appraisal of the stimulus predicts a change, an emotion will be generated. Depending on whether the change is expected to be positive or negative, the emotion will match.

The Appraisal Process:
  factors that affect how animals respond to things.

Novelty
  Suddenness, familiarity and predictability, and intrinsic pleasantness

Goal Significance
  Consequences of the stimulus relative to the animal's current needs and expectations

Coping Potential
  How well the animal can control and adapt to the event

Relevance to Norms
  Color added by the long term emotional habits of the animal (its personality)

Emotions modify perceptions and perceptions generate emotions. Perceptions will be more positive or negative under the influence of pre-existing emotions. Under the influence of negative emotions, it is easier for animals to memorize negative experiences. Emotion may directly alter the judgment or risk assessment process, or act indirectly through biases in the attention and memory processes that pertain to it. You can change perception by generating emotion. A good animal trainer will carefully and consciously condition and control emotional responses.

Current Known Emotional Systems Common to All Vertebrate Animals from Jaak Panksepp

- SEEKING (feels like enthusiasm)
- RAGE (feels like anger)
- FEAR (feels like anxiety)
- LUST (feels like wanting sex)
- CARE (feels like tender & loving)
- PANIC (feels like being painfully alone)
- PLAY (feels like joy)

Chapter 3

Neurochemistry, OMG!

The very idea of neurochemistry is enough to make some people go into an anxiety state. Relax, though, because this chapter has all the elements of a great movie: high tension, drama, desire, and sex. Lots of sex. It's just told at a little bit different level of detail than you are used to. Make some popcorn and sit back in your chair.

Fear (anxiety) is a stress emotion generated from the anticipation of harm. The stress response is a mechanism used by organisms to adapt to and overcome a stress stimulus in order to preserve homoeostasis. It supports survival. Anxiety is useful and necessary in moderation to overcome short term physical requirements (including emergencies).

General Fear-Related Behavior in All Vertebrate Animals

Internal
- heart rate elevation
- high levels of adrenaline
- increased circulating cortisol

External
- increased rate of defecation
- heightened vigilance
- momentary freezing and orienting
- increased speed of movement

The body responds to physical and psychological stress in the same way, although there are different initial pathways for stress. It may originate internally, in skin and muscles, as pain registered in the brain, or emotional distress. In response to any of these types of stress, the ancient defensive system immediately goes into action producing a number of key neurotransmitters.

How 2 Train A _____

> **Some Important Nervous System Chemicals**
> *at a glance with helpful rhymes*
>
> **Catecholamines** occur in the nerve system (*rhymes with "Cat is whole I means"*)
>   **Epinephrine** (a.k.a. Adrenaline) (*rhymes with "pep in F sin"*)
>   **Norepinephrine** (*rhymes with "No pep in F sin "*)
>   **Dopamine** (*rhymes with "Pope, I mean"*)
> **Opioids** occur in the nerve system (*rhymes with "oh, hemrrhoids!"*)
>   **Endorphins** (*rhymes with "Pen door fins"*)
> **Glucocorticoids** flow in the bloodstream (*rhymes with "screw no shorty droids"*)
>   **Cortisol** (*rhymes with "short is all"*)
> Sex and social bonding hormones
>   **Testosterone** (*rhymes with "Best foster bone"*)
>   **Estrogen** (*rhymes with "Best row, Men"*)
>   **Oxytocin**(*rhymes with "Moxy toes sin"*)
>   **Vasopressin** (*rhymes with "Say so dressin'"*)
>
> *Test your knowledge after reading this chapter by coming back and seeing if you can say something about what each one of these does.*
>
> **Please submit rhyme improvements on our website: www.How2TrainA. com with the subject: To the Attention of the Rhyme Improvement Department**

The two major classes of these compounds are catecholamines and glucocorticoids. Catecholamines include epinephrine (or adrenaline) and norepinephrine. The principal glucocorticoid is cortisol (related to the familiar cortisone). These three hormones enable the body to react to a perceived threat. Epinephrine increases blood pressure and heart rate, diverts blood to the muscles and speeds up reaction time. Norepinephrine is also involved with the response to threat and it plays an important role in vigilance and decision making. Cortisol releases sugar in the form of glucose from the body reserves to power the muscles and the brain into action. The catecholamines are considered to be involved with the need to be vigilant, while the glucocorticoids are involved with psychological discomfort that will ultimately cause the animal to seek change. Note though, that the system is complex and any one chemical might have various effects in various locations of the brain. I hate when I have to admit my description is merely a useful simplification.

The recall of memories is somewhat enhanced by stress, but learning is not. Recently researchers have shown that stress disrupts the process by which the brain collects, stores, and retrieves memories. Learning and memory take place at synapses, which are junctions through which nerve cells communicate. The neurotransmitters (opioids and the catchecolamines) carry messages across the synapse. These synapses reside on specialized branchlike protrusions on nerve cells called dendritic spines. The research showed that in the brain's primary learning and memory center, cortisol, which is not a neurotransmitter but circulates in the blood, leads to the rapid disintegration of these dendritic spines, which in turn limits the ability of synapses to collect and store memories. Other studies have shown that a small degree of stress may accelerate certain types of learning, but in general, we should assume that stress interferes with learning and storage of memory. Most animal trainers recognize that an agitated animal does not learn well, but now you know why!

Positive emotions have not been studied nearly as much as negative emotions. Very little is known about the chemistry of satisfaction, but the chemistry of motivation has received more attention. There appears to be at least two distinct classes of positive motivational states represented in the brain. An appetitive emotional system, devoted to foraging and reward-seeking, is dependent in part on the dopamine system. The second emotional system is involved in processing sensory pleasure, such as pleasurable touch and tastes. It involves the opioid system. Or, put more simply, dopamine reflects intensity of wanting while opioids determine what is wanted. Opioids stimulate the onset of motivated behavior, and activate the dopamine system. The dopamine system drives the expectation for reward and the willingness to work for reward. When the mad-scientists destroy the dopamine in some poor creature, there is no motivation to acquire food or mates even though there is normal enjoyment. Interestingly, dopamine belongs to the catecholamine family and is a precursor to adrenaline.

Brain opioid peptide systems are known to play an important role in motivation, emotion, attachment behavior, the response to stress and pain, and the control of food intake. Endorphin is a well-known opioid peptide that has analgesic effects similar to morphine. Stimulation of endorphin release is a goal of several horse training practices, including twitching (twisting the horse's nose). How odd that the system that controls our sense of pleasure can also be activated as an escape from pain!

Brain oxytocin together with vasopressin plays an important role in positive social bonding, triggering dopamine release to motivate social activities. Many studies have linked oxytocin, one of several mammalian hormones produced in the hypothalamus, to maternal bonding, trust and social recognition in several species. Social animals have a naturally high level of oxytocin, boosted in the species by their group dynamics, which can be exploited by bonding with an animal trainer. Oxytocin is needed to quiet the fear circuitry in their brains so that everyone and everything doesn't loom as a threat. With the fight/flight reflex in check, the animal is able to trust. For a trainer, it important to note that oxytocin release can be respondently conditioned. You can actually buy Oxytocin spray on the internet. It doesn't cross the barrier to the brain, but what would people want to use it for, if it did? Hint: they call it Liquid Trust.

Oxytocin is also very involved with the female reproductive system. It causes milk let down, contractions, and keeps the adverse aspects of labor and birthing from being lodged in the memory - and therein is the problem for training. It interferes with learning by punishment and negative reinforcement. Oxytocin also causes male erection, which may explain the male horses that drop their genitals in response to bonding activities with the humans and then seem to lose their ability to learn or focus. This seems to happen in about 2% of the animals we have trained, and we have learned to recognize it as a signal to make some changes in our training plans. Cortisol prevents erection.

Sex hormones are involved in the growth, maintenance, and repair of reproductive tissues. They also influence other body tissues and bone mass. The amount and levels of hormones change daily. The sex hormones, estrogen and testosterone, are secreted in short bursts -- pulses -- which vary from hour to hour and even minute to minute.

Estrogen is an entire class of related hormones. While most estrogen is produced in the female reproductive tissues, some is also produced by the liver, in the breasts, in the adrenal glands, and in fat cells. Low or fluctuating estrogen can cause anxiety or depression.

It appears that two different mechanisms are at work to insure the appropriate expression of maternal behavior. One is mediated by the fetus during pregnancy and the other is associated with the oxytocin release that occurs at parturition. These regulate the various functions associated with motherhood including protection of the babies. Mammalian mothers tend to aggressively guard their offspring for a short period, and then gradually grow lax. However, working with a mother-baby pair can create a challenge for a trainer.

Testosterone levels of both males and females vary widely. Testosterone does not cause aggression, but it releases the aggressive urges from inhibition. Young males usually do not show testosterone related behaviors, but as a male matures he is less inhibited from showing aggressive behaviors if they are there. Testosterone and fear make a very potent combination. When working with intact male horses, we work through a fence panel until the animal is not fearful. The problems are much more apparent during breeding season. Despite their popular image, stallions are not brave (they hide behind the mares) and act more like fear-biting dogs!

The power of social drive in social animals is often overlooked. Their evolutionary history has saddled them with a neurochemical system that is very sensitive to the dynamics of social inclusion. Scientists are suggesting that the emotional result of social rejection is neurochemically the same emotional "hurt" as physical injury. You may be hurting your animal with social rejection every bit as much as if you were slapping them! This has very important significance for animal trainers. Being your animal's best friend has advantages.

Few trainers give much thought to the neurochemical changes they create in their animals. But if you hold this paradigm in mind, the emotional arousal of your animal becomes something you can manipulate for the good.

Chapter 4

A Few Extra Words about Fear

"It was a dark and stormy night; the rain fell in torrents-- except at occasional intervals, when it was checked by a violent gust of wind which swept up the streets (for it is in London that our scene lies), rattling along the housetops, and fiercely agitating the scanty flame of the lamps that struggled against the darkness."
    --Edward George Bulwer-Lytton, *Paul Clifford (1830)*

For just a moment, stop and think about a time you were really afraid for your safety. What does that feel like? Are you one of those people who avoids scaring yourself, or do you go out of your way to read a scary book or watch a horror film? What allows us to tie fear and fun together in an emotional experience?

Most fear, however, is quite grim. It's a gut level sense of terror. It's hard to write about without sensing the oppression. For the animal, who has no way of knowing what we might have planned for it, fears can be very overwhelming.

Since we can only guess about the subjective emotions of an animal, we need to agree that "fear" refers to the activation of the defensive behavioral system that responds to perception of danger. We will never know what it actually feels like to an animal, but we can't say they don't experience it.

Fearful experiences are critical events in the training of any animal, but especially in the training of a non-domestic animal. Fright speeds the learning of escape behaviors and converts the lesson into long term memory very rapidly. Something learned under stress is more likely to be retained, but unless you have prevented every possible evasion, what is likely to be learned is something you don't want the animal to learn. We could train without fear in a perfect world, but on this planet, we will have to resign ourselves to constantly strive for a least fearful scenario.

Fears can be divided into two general classes: **learned** and **unlearned**. Unlearned fear is naturally provoked even when the animal has had no prior experience with the stimulus. Unlearned fears arise from such things as their natural predators (including humans), erratic and unpredictable stimuli, and exposure to a novel place (especially one that is brightly lighted or elevated). Conditioned or learned fear is provoked by stimuli that have become associated with something aversive. Fear of whips or ropes is conditioned by pairing the object with a bad experience and is not innate to the animal. Conditioned fear stimuli provoke the same behaviors that innate fear stimuli provoke.

"Here's Johnny!!"
--Jack Nicholson, *The Shining (1980)*

How do you recognize fear? It creates profound changes in the physiological condition of the animal. Defecation and liquidity of feces increase and blood pressure shows a reliable increase. Heart rate is less consistent than the hypertensive effects of fear stimuli. Both tachycardia (fast pulse) and bradycardia (slowed pulse) have been reported under various conditions, especially restraint. Animals snort, open their noses and eyes wide, and raise their heads. There is an associated loss in pain sensitivity. The animals' body is going into survival mode.

To measure the fear, specific responses can be quantified such as fear-potentiated startle, freezing, head elevation, nose flaring, and snorting. With a heart rate monitor, tachycardia or bradycardia can be measured. Variability of the heart rate decreases with fear as the defense system locks the heart into maximum readiness. Fear can also be measured by disruption of normal behaviors, this measure is called **suppression**. Later in the book, you will see why you might want to measure fear responses.

While fight and flight are the most common responses to the perception of danger, there is another response put into service by some horsetrainers. Other animal trainers are typically astounded by this somewhat common method. To understand it, we need to look briefly at the defense system itself. The amygdalae (a deep ancient part of the brain) plays the central role in the acquisition and expression of learned fears. The amygdalae are the interface between the sensory system, which perceives the danger, and the different motor and autonomic systems that control the response to that danger. The autonomic nervous system has two branches which can be activated: 1) the **sympathetic**, emergency **fight-or-flight** system, and 2) the **parasympathetic** withdrawal/immobility system. Under normal conditions the parasympathetic nervous system facilitates homeostatic functions such as digestion, growth, healing, and conservation of energy. The parasympathetic nervous system's second function kicks into operation when the sympathetic nervous system's fight-or-flight operations fail. This causes a sudden, massive parasympathetic response and the animal may collapse into immobility.

Let me explain that in another way. If the animal perceives danger when it can do something to respond, it causes a fight or flight response. If it cannot hide, fight, or flee, it may be thrust into a system shutdown and collapse into immobility. It falls down and lies as if dying. The old style of horse training relying on methods to subjugate them or lay them on the ground evoked the parasympathic response to immobilize the animal. The result was a window of a few hours when the horse would not engage in fight or flight behaviors, a window in which the horse-trainers tried to habituate the horse to being ridden. The problem with this procedure is that it may create anxiety disorders that are not understood yet in animals. In humans it creates Post Traumatic Stress Disorder.

Another important phenomenon of fear is the **startle reflex** (SR). This innate behavior is a fast twitch of facial and body muscles triggered by a sudden sound, feel, or sight. The actual base reflex is that the eyes close, the muscles in the neck and shoulders contract, other behavior stops, and the heart rate goes up. You see it when babies are suddenly frightened. The next step for most animals is a jump away from the offending stimulus (but babies can't jump yet). Clearly the behaviors are going to contribute to survival of the animals in the face of danger. Startle can be elicited from almost any animal species.

Things that influence the startle reflex:
- Stimulus intensity
- Ongoing activity
- Animal personality
- Sensory environment
- Background noise
- Light

In situations where the animal already feels threatened, the startle reflex is more easily triggered. This is called **Fear-Potentiated Startle Response** (FPSR). Normal sudden sounds trigger panic responses when they happen to an already adrenalized animal. The animal farts and scares itself. The triggers for fear are additive. Panic behavior sets in as the animal's survival instincts sacrifice any level of coordination and planning for a quick response. The training session seems to be going downhill, and it is, certainly, because the animal is operating from fear rather than from understanding.

Some individual animals (including people) have nervous systems wired for very low thresholds for the startle response under any conditions, and some are pushed into pathological anxiety by experience. Research for animal models to study Post Traumatic Stress Disorder has shown that there are many variations of genetic factors that can cause temperamentally fearful animals. One of the surest ways for the researchers to produce anxious dispositions for their research is to remove the baby animal from it's mother. This creates a permanently anxious laboratory animal.

Although fleeing danger often provides the best chance for an animal's survival, when escape is not possible, aggression often minimizes the likelihood of injury or death. Physical pain elicits unconditioned aggression because pain frequently indicates a situation that requires immediate action. Thus, pain frequently triggers behavior that is quick and highly reactive, as when a bee sting triggers frantic attempts to swat at the bee. In this way, if aggression is effective at eliminating the danger, it can be a reinforced behavior, allowing us to predict that aggressive responses will become more frequent. You are likely to engage in frantic attempts to swat at the bee *before* it stings the next time.

Pain signals reach reflexive motor circuits in the brain before the pain is consciously realized, so responses to aversive stimuli may not be as much of a decision as a habitual action.

A surge of adrenaline can also be experienced as a very positive experience. Besides the horror movie phenomenon, consider the case of extreme sports. It's a rush. It's a rush for animals as well, and they can access adrenaline though escape or aggressive behaviors. The more your animal practices these kinds of behaviors, the more likely it is to become "addicted" to the adrenaline high. Give these "fast trigger" animals plenty of time and space to cavort with their companions to burn up that adrenaline but keep training sessions calm and quiet.

Many bad behaviors are expressions of the flight response. Any level of tension signaling potential flight will detract from the ability of the animal to learn things other than flight behaviors. Any perceptions the animal has under tension will be colored by stress hormones. No matter what kind of training style you use, a relaxed animal is much more open to learning and remembering. The only way out of fear is to replace the neurochemistry of fear with the neurochemistry of well-being. It's a big job, but we have some tools to help..

Chapter 5

Methods to Eliminate Fear

Now that we have looked at what fear is, we can think about how to get rid of it. Forgetting is not an option; once trained, and without further manipulation, conditioned fear lasts a lifetime, essentially unchanged from the moment it was acquired.

Habituation is the change in the animal's response due to repeated presentation. When a stimulus fails to predict anything of importance to the animal, it becomes irrelevant. Present the signal repeatedly without any consequence to the animal and the animal will soon learn to ignore the signal. Watch a worried animal carefully to see what sets off suspicious, fearful behavior. If you can isolate the signals for fear into very small packets and habituate to them, you can get the animal working in a positive frame of mind. You can't desensitize an animal to all future stimuli, but you can work on what is bothering them right now to create a positive frame of mind where the need to flee is diminished.

The Dual-Process Theory of Habituation says that habituation (becoming less aware) and sensitization (becoming more aware) are continuously opposing processes that are constantly being balanced by the central nervous system. An animal trainer needs a balance of sensitization and desensitization. The animal needs to be sensitized to cues and desensitized to random and irrelevant stimuli.

Extinction is the loss of a learned behavior as a result of repeated non-reinforcement for the behavior. The previously learned evasive behavior no longer reinforced, and the behavior diminishes (is extinguished). Unfortunately, fear itself is totally resistant to extinction. Once an animal is taught to fear something, the fear doesn't go away. But it can learn that running away is not the way to solve the problem.

Conditioned Inhibition is a stimulus paired with the absence of an aversive event. Something becomes a signal that an aversive event won't happen. This principle can be exploited for training social animals. Having another friendly calm animal that the animal trainee knows can help to keep the trainee calm through a training session. The calmness of the friendly animal is a signal that there is no danger. Walking into the pen with food will result in less fear than walking into the pen empty handed because the food signals your intent. The time of day is often a signal the animals are attuned to, allowing you to approach much closer and showing little fear at feeding time. If you are training with pressure, consistently using safety signals can greatly enhance training.

Latent Inhibition is an inconsequential presentation of the prospective stimulus before training which results in the stimulus not being perceived as significant during training. This does not decrease fear except in a proactive way. It is hard to form emotional memories about common place things. For reduction of fear, this principle says if the animal learns that it is an irrelevant stimulus, it is not later likely to develop a fear of it. But it will be more difficult to sensitize the animal to it if later you want the animal to respond to it. An example of this is what happens to your ability to "herd" an animal as it grows comfortable about you. It becomes much easier to lead an animal when it is used to its handler, because chasing just doesn't work anymore.

A **preparatory signal** is a distinctive non-startling signal presented just before a startling stimulus. This type of signal will reduce the magnitude of the startle response. We use this principle by saying "Ready!" before we offer a cue, touch the animal, or even if we know something is about to make a loud sound. It seems odd, but using a loud voice to alert to a impending crash, keeps the noise from scaring the animal as much.

Just as an unpleasant situation increases the startle reflex, a **pleasant situation** will decrease the startle reflex. If the animal is under the influence of happy emotions, it will take a bigger stimulus to set off a startle.

Counter-conditioning (perception modification) based in respondent conditioning is used by appetitive-based trainers. A stimulus with a negative perception can be paired with food or other desirable rewards and it will become a predictor of good things. Suddenly that scary thing is very interesting to the animal. People instinctively do this when they follow an innate drive to offer a frightened wild animal some food. Chapter 14 addresses respondent conditioning.

Chapter 6

Like a snowflake.

Although every animal obeys the Laws of Behavior, every animal has its own distinct personality. No two animals are exactly alike. The more animals you train, the clearer this fact becomes. There can be no one-size-fits-all recipe for training. Their personalities might be colored by transient factors like nutrient levels, hormonal states, or they may reflect longer term coping styles that they learned early in life. Even after you train hundreds of animals, you will still find yourself being surprised by their individual quirks.

The age of the animal makes a difference in the ease of training for many species. Juvenile animals are generally more willing to take direction. Most species of domestic animals retain their juvenile attitude (a phenomenon called neotony) which keeps them more willing to comply with our wishes. Our ancestors probably ate the animals with a less willing attitude! Exotic animals grow up mentally and become less tractable as they mature. So even the snowflake aspect of the individual is but a transient snapshot of the whole animal personality.

There is nothing you can do to avoid it, you must engage with the animal as an individual. Observe the behaviors in which this creature freely engages -- this is going to provide you with a good idea of what your animal friend will find rewarding. What does this particular animal like to do? Where does it like to be? We will be needing this information soon.

Chapter 7

The Ethical Trainer

Ethical Dilemma

The world of horse training exists in complete contradiction to all of the values esteemed in Applied Animal Behavior training. Taken at face value, horse training must be a dismal failure according to what the textbooks predict will happen when **aversive** stimulation is used. Furthermore, in the Companion Animal-training World, the gurus say novices should not even be taught to use those techniques because it will only bring suffering to animals. Yet in horse training, those techniques, generally referred to as pressure/release, are ubiquitous.[1]

Because other methods are so successful, contemporary science-based trainers, with few exceptions, do not use pressure/release methods, which rely on aversive motivation. The applied science trainers often know only the rudiments of how to use pressure, which they have been exposed to as compulsion training for dogs. Meanwhile, although these principles are described in the laws of behavior, the horse world has little access to relevant material written from a scientific basis. The result is that there are two worlds of training that don't speak each other's language.

Furthermore, the market for horse training information is dominated by some colorful personalities with huge advertising budgets, compared to which applied behavior science is almost invisible. The scientific terminology occasionally gets put into service to establish some level of credibility for horse-trainers, but it is almost always used incorrectly. I want to give horse trainers a chance to understand their work from a scientific perspective, to put that vocabulary and its related concepts within their reach. The risk is that novices will learn the

---

1   I am happy to note that this has greatly improved between the time of first and second publication. Positive reinforcement now has a foothold in horse training.

"dangerous" pressure techniques. Meanwhile there are 100's of Natural Horsemanship clinicians line up to teach them pressure! I believe that the horse-training community needs the concepts and language to critically think about pressure/release.

Making Ethical Decisions:

> **The Six Pillars of Character**
> From the Josephson Institute
> **Trustworthiness**.
> > Honesty,
> > > Honesty in communications:
> > > > truthfulness,
> > > > sincerity,
> > > > candor
> > > Honesty in conduct
> > Integrity,
> > Reliability (promise-keeping)
> > Loyalty
> **Respect**: Do unto others as you would have them do unto you.
> > Civility, Courtesy and Decency
> > Dignity and Autonomy
> > Tolerance and Acceptance
> **Responsibility**.
> > Accountability
> > Pursuit of Excellence
> > Self-Restraint
> **Fairness**.
> > Adherence to Process for Justice
> > Impartiality
> > Equity
> **Caring**.
> > Do no harm other than what is necessary
> **Citizenship**.
> > A good citizen gives more than she takes.

Use this book wisely. Use it to improve what you are doing now and use it to pick out the best possible way to solve your problems as they arise. Use it to do the least harm. Use it to enrich the lives of animals.

The two fundamental ethical questions must be asked.

1. Who do we want to be?

I believe that working with animals gives you a mirror to see yourself. Because they reflect our energies and respond to what we do, not what we say, the animal can only respond to our authentic selves. They provide honest feedback if we want to instigate changes in our character and demeanor.

I believe that animals respond favorably to the same qualities of human character that people value. Certainly, they are keen judges of our trustworthiness, our fairness, the respect we offer them, and the care we give them.

2. How should this animal be treated?

The English Farm Animal Welfare Council has published the Five Freedoms that all English farm animals are due:

- **Freedom from Hunger and Thirst** - by ready access to fresh water and a diet to maintain full health and vigour.
- **Freedom from Discomfort** - by providing an appropriate environment including shelter and a comfortable resting area.
- **Freedom from Pain, Injury or Disease** - by prevention or rapid diagnosis and treatment.
- **Freedom to Express Normal Behaviour** - by providing sufficient space, proper facilities and company of the animal's own kind (for social animals).
- **Freedom from Fear and Distress** - by conditions and treatment which avoid mental suffering.

No matter what else you believe, you must afford your animals the same basic "freedoms". These things are not controversial.

What is controversial is the use of aversives to get the creatures to do our bidding. In horse training it is called "pressure". In theory, this pressure could be only mildly annoying, but in practice the aversiveness can be rapidly escalated if the animal ignores it. In the Parelli horse-training system the metaphor is that it is in stages, equivalent to sequentially: a fly; a mosquito; a blackbird; and an eagle. The eagle does whatever it takes to get the horse to comply. Some horse-trainers recommend steady but annoying pressure, but the novice trying to figure out what is correct protocol is more likely to encounter the more pervasive "get 'er done" guidance. The animal is "rewarded" for compliance with a "release" of this pressure. There is no logical boundary between tapping the animal rhythmically with a whip and beating it with a club, so people go to extremes thinking they are supposed to do it that way. "Get 'er done!!!" All kinds of unnecessary physical abuses take place in the name of training. No wonder we animal trainers are never quite trusted!

The history of animal's rights is incredibly interesting as the story of human's evolution of character. It has generally been expedient for humans to denigrate their status to mere beasts who have no feelings. Perhaps these ideas enhance the fitness of the culture which can efficiently exploit the animals without remorse? When the cultural belief was that man was given dominion over the animals and that animals were a blessing God gave to our species, we became pretty bad roommates on this small planet.

In the 1600's the Church/State started losing power over the individual. People started questioning things that had always been taken for granted as science began to have more accurate predictive power than the Church. Personal responsibility took hold in the collective consciousness and people started developing personal ethics. I believe that Animal Rights grew out of the concept of personal responsibility. By the 1800's animal protection laws were beginning. The story of Animal Rights continues to unfold. The modern middle of the road concept is that the ability to suffer, not the ability to reason, should be the benchmark of how we treat other beings. As trainers, we have a responsibility to set personal policies as to how much suffering we will impose on our wards.

Trainers will naturally be in conflict with those who propose that humans should mind their own business and leave the poor animals in peace. We can, however, aspire to train with the least aversive method possible. The reality, though, is that aversives are a natural part of life and every animal is prepared to cope with a reasonable level of them. Don't you suspect that human life without aversives might be extremely boring and we might have to invent some problems just to keep ourselves entertained? The bottom line for many trainers is how efficiently the animals can be trained and how reliable the behaviors are.

Other trainers only enjoy their work if they believe that they are enriching their animals' lives. There are many ways to see it.

In the end, we have to decide for ourselves who we want to be. Yes, we are back to personal responsibility.

Chapter 8

Animal Welfare Notes

Recognizing Problems

The emergence of animal welfare as a science has highlighted some areas of disconnection between humans and their animals. Careless performance of routine animal husbandry practices most certainly contribute to animals becoming fearful of people. It has been well documented that livestock handlers, out of tradition, ignorance, and negative attitudes, are frequently responsible for aversive experiences of their own livestock causing undue stress and depressing productivity. Just because someone has livestock experience does not qualify them as an expert in animal welfare. Believe your own observations and take action to correct situations where animals are being taught to fear humans. You may be the only one that will speak for the animal.

Human behaviors that can contribute to animal fear:

- Unwanted touching of the animal;
- Hitting the animal;
- Use of a flag, prod or rope to move the animal;
- Shouting;
- Standing on an elevated position;
- Moving fast;
- Appearing suddenly;
- Chasing the animal or otherwise behaving as a predator;
- Rough, aversive and/or unpredictable handling;
- Moving erratically; and
- Banging gates, feed troughs, or other things.

Fear of humans creates numerous problems for animals. Animals can be injured or killed (ie. breaking their necks) trying to avoid or escape humans. Acute or chronic fear can predispose the animal to immunosuppressant disorders or colic, while there is no possibility of treating a sick animal without adding to the fear level. A panicked large animal poses a distinct danger to any humans in the confines of the pen. Out of their own fears, people often respond to fearful animals in ways that frighten the animal even more. Fearful animals are not attractive to people and people find less reason to treat the not-so-cute animal with compassion.. Overcoming fear is difficult.

Evidence of a positive environment include fewer agonistic displays (any social behavior related to fighting), occasional displays of play behaviors, quiet movements without running into the fence, absence of snorting, and evidence of curiosity. Extreme calmness, however, can be a sign of depression or learned helplessness.

In all mammals, the "startle reflex" is easier to trigger in an emotional backdrop of stress hormones. A low threshold for this behavior, which most people call jumpiness, can be a signal that the animal is stressed or that the individual animal has a low threshold for stress. It is worthwhile to track the frequency of startle responses during training. Note what you were training the animal to do, what the proximate cause of the startle was, and any background factors that might have added an element of distraction or anxiety. Patterns will emerge.

Heart rate increases in response to negative perceptions, but it can also increase in anticipation of reward. Heart rate variability (HRV) is thought to be a better measure of stress/pleasure, where HRV decreases under stress but not under pleasure. There is more variability in the heart rate of a contented animal because it is not under control by the alert system of nerves, which maximizes efficiency in preparation for response to threat. The technology to measure HRV is affordable..

Promoting Positive Emotions

There are five ways we promote positive emotions at our training facility.

Signaling or predicting a reward in advance. The period

between the signal that food is coming and the arrival of the food merits close inspection. This is when anticipatory behaviors are expressed. When your animal calls to you to bring his food, you have crossed the threshold beyond being merely a source of fear. It helps if the food delivery is totally predictable at first. If the animal finds the process chaotic and unpredictable, aggression comes out and food may be grabbed. In later stages, making the food less predictable is used to keep boredom from setting in, but until boredom seems possible, look for ways to increase predictability.

Giving a higher reward than expected. Positive contrast and **negative contrast** are behavioral effects of changing the size of the reward. Once the animal has its expectations set, decreasing the size of the reward will result in the animal putting less effort in to the successive trials, while increasing the size of the reward will result in the animal putting more effort into the successive trials. It's not about the absolute magnitude of the reward, but rather the discrepancy between the expectation and the reward given. The resulting emotion of a jackpot sized reward seems akin to joy or elation.

Enabling the animals to cope with or to control the situation. Giving the animal a sense of control over its environment is an important source of positive emotions. If the animal is always presented with a choice and the results are predictable to the animal, the animal will be less stressed. Even if the results are negative, the very existence of a choice makes the results more palatable to the animal. Negative reinforcement can be perceived as positive when there are clear opportunities for avoidance. Frequent challenges, that can always be successfully mastered and eventually enable the animal to reach a desired and rewarding goal, are a way to regularly evoke positive emotions.

Providing an enriched environment. A complex habitat is better than a featureless corral. Provision of a hiding place and interesting companions help calm social animals. If a animal has to be separated from his family, providing diversionary companions seems to prevent depression. In a caged environment, being able to socialize through the wire is important. Feeding in containers that make the animal work for its food gives the animal something to be occupied with. Opening the cages and letting the animals roam and explore helps them accept their life in captivity. Providing a large space to run with companions, water to paw, and sand to roll in are things to make life better for many species. Animal environmental enrichment is a fast growing field with many developing web resources.

Prepare for necessary aversive events. Getting back on to the horsetrailer, going to the vet, having strangers handle the animal are all unavoidable potentially aversive eventualities. By taking the time to associate drills of these activities with positive rewards, the emotions generated at the real event will be much less negative. We feed in the horsetrailer, do pretend veterinary procedures just for practice, and get anyone available to give our horses a positive perspective on strangers.

Animal-Human Relationships

It is clear that an animal's perception of humans is based on its history of interactions with them. They may appraise us as anything from dangerous predators to safety signals. Luckily for us, animals differentiate between people for the most part, and the animal will have a specific relationship with each of us. As a trainer, an animal may behave perfectly for you, but you may never be able to patch up a relationship between an animal and an owner without the owner making a huge commitment to change. The Laws of Behavior work on animal owners too.

Chapter 9

Laws of Behavior: the Core Concepts

Finally, we have arrived at the Laws of Behavior. This is the heart and soul of informed animal training. All the animal training that has ever been done (even if by other animals) was done according to these laws. Figuring out how to describe your current training methods in this language is the first step. Then look around and see what else you can put in your training toolbox.

You're going to be able to compare different methods in meaningful ways. When you master this section you are well on your way to being literate in the field of Applied Behavior Analysis. Reading the technical literature or attending a conference in the field will be doable.

Please do not read it all at once. For best retention of this material read a couple of pages and then go do something else (training an animal would be excellent!). Come back later and review, then go on to the next few pages. Play with it! The more fun you have with it, the better you will remember it.

1. The Scientific Approach to Changing Behavior

Laws of Behavior are as reliable as the Laws of Gravity.

1.1. Science is based on the principle of **Determinism**, which holds behavior is lawful, caused by events in the physical world, and it is possible to discover and benefit from understanding these laws. Training animals involves cause and effect in the physical world, which can be described with laws. No magic is needed.

1.2. The goals of **Behavior Analysis** are to discover basic behavioral principles, establish generality of the principles, and develop an applied technology based on these principles. Training animals is the application of behavior principles to modify behavior.

1.3. The value of **Pragmatism** holds that truth is defined in terms of the predictability and control it provides. Using this criteria, a concept is "more true" if it provides better prediction and control of behavior. A training system is better if it gives the trainer more control. Animal trainers are interested in results!

1.4. **Behavior analysis** is a natural science that seeks to understand the behavior of individuals. Behavior analysts focus on the individual because behavior is done by individuals. Their goal is to understand the factors that reliably influence behavior usually to cause the acquisition of new behaviors or the decrease of problem behaviors..

1.5. Other Approaches to Understanding Learning

>1.5.1. **Cognitive learning** is a form of altering behavior that involves higher mental processes such as rational thinking. While many animal trainers value rational thinking, they always find that interpreting their animal's actions is easier than interpreting their thoughts.
>
>1.5.2. **Mentalism** holds that an inner dimension (black box) which lies outside realm of physical phenomena exists. The concerns of mentalism (thoughts, beliefs, values, etc.) are left to other branches of psychology. Behaviorists feel that mentalism unnecessarily complicates the analysis of behavior and obscures the actual measurable causes of behavior. Animal trainers do not care if there is a black-box. We are pragmatic.
>
>1.5.3. There is a quasi-holistic model of behavior says that everything is in harmony until some part of it breaks down and needs to be fixed. The question asked under this model is "What do you or your animal need to bring your life back into order?" Problems are interpreted as system malfunctions which can be diagnosed and fixed. Most non-scientific animal training advice is made on the

basis of this model. The diagnoses are things like "lacks respect" and "stubborn". Adding some respect or getting rid of the stubbornness are problematic training goals. Animal trainers know that you can't teach an animal something that will magically make it understand and perform all other desirable behaviors. Animal trainers know you have to train one behavior at a time and they are adept at motivating their trainees. Concepts like respect and stubbornness become irrelevant.

1.5.4. Applying a label to the inner dimensions of your animal to explain its behavior creates confusion. Behaviorists recommend that you restrain yourself to a simple description of observable events. They select the simplest possible explanation for how and why an animal performs a behavior. They work from a list of the actual behaviors the animal performs and doesn't perform, rather than from an interpretation of the animal personality. Animal trainers look for what needs to be trained next.

1.5.5. Inserting human level thoughts into the mind of an animal is frowned upon. It is not scientific and if you do it, it should be done in the spirit of a cartoonist rather than a behaviorist. The cat comes running when you open the refrigerator because he knows the milk is in there? No! Don't say it that way! The opening of the refrigerator door is a signal that milk may soon be available. Meow!

1.5.6. Behavior can also be studied from an **ethological model** which holds that behavior is a result of adaptations of a species to its natural habitat. These adaptations improve the animals' chances for survival and reproduction. The ethological and behavioral models are inseparable for animal trainers because how an animal responds to training, depends on the biological adaptations of its species. Animal trainers want to, as much as possible, do what comes natural to the animal. Animals are amazing to begin with.

Chapter 10

2. Behavior: Stimulus – Response Relationships

Dead Animal Test: You know it's a behavior if a dead animal can't do it.

2.1. **Behaviors** can involve observable physical movements or private events that only take place in the nervous system of the animal. Behaviorists prefer to work with overt measurable behaviors. Trying to measure the immeasurable is a topic for later in this book.

2.2. Behaviorists refer to dependent relations as a **contingency**. Anything that has an "if-then" relationship is called a contingency. A **contingency statement** is a formal way to make an if-then statement. An example of this would be "if it is raining, then it must be cloudy." Rainy is contingent upon cloudy. In most cases, animal trainers are interested in a statement containing two contingency statements that are linked by the result of the second one being dependent upon the first one. Something triggers a behavior, and then the behavior results in a consequence. Memorize that sentence. It really is that simple.

The factors that triggered the behavior in the first place are called **antecedents**. Because we aren't certain about what is going on in the animals mind, the antecedents contain all the pre-existing circumstances. This includes both the immediate trigger and all of the environmental factors that provide a context for the animal. The immediate trigger is called the **discriminative stimuli** and the contextual factors are called **function-altering stimuli**.

The circumstances which follow the behavior are called **postcedents**. It is *only* if a postcedent can be shown to influence future behavior that it is called a **consequence**. People make careers of using these fancy words for very simple ideas. They study **functional relationships**, which means they try to quantify the relationship between the behaviors, the triggers, and the consequences within a set of contingencies.

Postcedents turn into antecedents for the next behavior!!!
All animal organisms live in a continuous flow of antecedent conditions which they continuously respond to.

Training is basically controlling the postcedent environment in ways that increase or decrease the likelihood that an animal will perform the behavior in the future. Animal trainers parse time into antecedents, behaviors, and consequences. They talk about the A,B,Cs.

Contingencies of Particular Interest to Animal Trainers:

Antecedents --> Behaviors --> Postcedents

Antecedents = { Discriminative Stimuli + Function Altering Stimuli }
Postcedents = { Consequences affecting subsequent behaviors + Inconsequential aspects }

40   How 2 Train A _____

2.2.1.

The CONTINGENCY Challenge: For each panel in the comic below, as you look at it for the first time, identify the behavior shown. What are the antecedents in each panel, and what are the postcedents? Notice how the antecedents flow. In a strict contingency analysis, you would identify the behavior first and look at the consequences, before you tried to analyze the antecedents, however in a story setting, that is almost impossible because the antecedents are the story.

Grindstone George a comic from April 05,1918: "Locked out, then knocked out."

2.2.2. Contingency Statement: **Antecedents -> Behaviors -> Consequences**

(Heads up: that will be on the final exam!)

Once you are able to put behavior into a contingency statement, you can start making predictions based on the consequences.

Example: You see stuffed meatballs on the menu-->You order it -->It gives you indigestion.

Prediction: you are not likely to order stuffed meatballs again.

ps. Things can get a lot more complicated than that for humans, but rarely for animals.

2.2.2.1. There are a few factors that make contingencies easier or harder to learn from.

- **Consistency**: the strictness of the if-then relationship. If the result is always the same, it is easier to learn.
- **Contiguity**: the closeness in time and space between cause and result. If the result occurs milliseconds after the antecedent condition, the animal is more likely to

learn from the association.

- **Frequency**: the number of times the condition and result are paired. If the cause has resulted in that outcome over and over, the animal is more likely to learn the relationship.

2.2.3. A **stimulus** is anything capable of influencing behavior. It can be tangible or intangible. It does not need to influence behavior to be a stimulus, but if it doesn't influence behavior it is called a **neutral stimulus**.

2.2.3.1. There are usually numerous stimuli impacting the organism at any one moment, but behaviorists focus on the most salient one. With experience, the animal trainer becomes aware of more stimuli influencing the results. The animal is aware of many more stimuli than the trainer can perceive.

2.2.3.2. A **neutral stimulus** can become a non-neutral stimulus and influence behavior. It is helpful to identify one slated for this change as a pre-stimulus. Pre-stimuli become stimuli. How simple is that?

2.2.3.3. Conditioned vs Unconditioned. An **unconditioned stimulus** elicits a certain predictable response typically without previous training. A **conditioned stimulus** was a neutral pre-stimulus before training, but now elicits a certain predictable response. In our everyday lives, icons are a conditioned stimulus that is intended to bring a commercial product to mind. A business carefully chooses the icon to represent their company. A golden arch was once a neutral stimulus, now what does it signify?

2.2.3.4. Aversive vs Appetitive. **Aversive** stimuli are ones that organisms would rather avoid. Aversive stimuli are appraised as annoying, painful, and noxious. Strongly aversive stimuli produce anxiety, panic and fear. Many things are inherently aversive because organisms that avoid them have higher survival rates. Novelty and unpredictability are innately unpleasant to most animals. Animals generally do not like being exposed in an open area where they have no cover to hide. Animals get frustrated when they can't get access to things normally available to them. Just because it is not aversive to our minds, does not mean that it is non-aversive to an animal.

Paying attention to your animal will help you understand what he/she finds aversive.

Appetitive stimuli are the ones organisms seek out. They are often the things necessary to sustain life and maintain homeostasis. Or they may simply be fun and pleasant. Examples of appetitive stimuli are food, water, temperature control, safety, social interaction, sex, etc. Over time, we are conditioned to add more things to our list of personal appetitive stimuli. You might find cute, fuzzy animals on your list.

2.2.3.5. Internal (**endogenous**) vs External (**exogenous**). Some stimuli are occurring in the black box of your mind. If they are working inside the mind, then they are endogenous. A cup of coffee in the morning might stimulate a lot of behavior. A belly full of turkey might stimulate a long afternoon nap. The presence of analgesic neurochemicals in your bloodstream instead of adrenalin, might explain that sleepy look on your face. Wake up! Pay attention!! (Sorry, I hope that I didn't scare you…). Me yelling is an exogenous stimulus.

2.2.3.5.1. People and animals may be unconsciously sensitive to the emotional state of other people and animals. Anxiety in the trainer may be a stimulus for anxiety of the animal. These things could be transmitted by either unconscious body language or through pheromones. Without a vomeronasal organ, we may never know. If you are nervous or upset, it is best to avoid the training pen.

2.2.3.6. Appraisal of stimuli is relative. Warmth may be an appetitive stimulus when it is cold, but an aversive stimulus when it is hot. Sex may be an appetitive stimulus for an 18 year old male, but an aversive stimulus for another human with a different state of mind. Food gets kind of unappealing after a big meal. It all depends!

2.2.3.7. **Biological Preparedness**: Any quality of the environment may be important for survival and animals may have sensory systems to detect patterns and changes associated with that quality of the environment. Humans have 5 basic senses: touch, taste, smell, hearing, and sight with which to detect and respond to the biologically relevant signals around them. Many more sensory systems are known from

How 2 Train A _____   43

other species that respond to magnetic fields, electrical fields, and sonar. It is hard for humans to imagine the experience of a sensory system we don't possess. Compared to what is possible, humans have a narrow range of sensory capacity in each of the sensory systems we do have. We don't hear the ultra-sound, see the infra-red or ultra-violet, or consciously smell the pheromones that are prominent parts of other animals' worlds. Our sensory systems are depauperate compared to the taste and smell systems of most animals. The only really good news for humans is that we see better in daylight than most mammals. The importance of this is that we do not inhabit the same sensory world as the animals we train. We don't have a way to see what they see, smell what they smell, or hear what they hear. Our experience of the world is limited and it helps the animal trainer to remain conscious of that fact.

2.2.3.8. **Stimulus Control**: Cues and Signals. A stimulus becomes a cue or signal by acquiring meaning that is salient to the animal. It provides the animal with information about what rules are in play. A stimulus that signals that a specific behavior will be reinforced or punished is called the **discriminative stimulus** (SD) or the **cue**. There are semantic arguments about calling these salient stimuli "cues" or "signals", but if you have a lot of animals to train, you don't have time to argue semantics endlessly. When the training is strong enough that presenting the SD results in the behavior every time, the behavior is said to be under stimulus control (or on cue).

2.2.3.9. **Discrimination** is the ability to respond differently to distinct stimuli. The animal learns to differentiate between stimuli, recognizing which is signaling for a particular response. Humans learning to drive are taught to discriminate between the shapes and colors of different traffic signs. A red octagon is a discriminative stimulus to stop.

2.2.3.10. **Generalization** is the ability of a broad class of stimuli to elicit the same response: A generalization gradient occurs when stimuli are increasingly different than the discriminative stimulus results in a gradient of behavior reduction. The variety of cell phone ringtones reflects our willingness to respond with the same behavior even if the stimulus is different.

2.2.3.11. **Fading** is not what happens to old stimuli. Rather, fading a stimulus involves transferring stimulus control to a new stimulus or to gradually change the antecedent stimulus in some respect, usually making it much less noticeable. This will be discussed in a later chapter.

2.2.4. A **response** is a reaction to a stimulus or a specific instance of behavior.

2.2.4.1. Conditioned vs Unconditioned. **Unconditioned responses** are an organism's automatic (or natural) reaction to a stimulus. Examples of this include running away when afraid, a newborn's search for it mothers udders, and salivating when you see or smell something nice to eat.

2.2.4.2. **Appetitive behaviors** function to obtain and secure desirable stimuli. It can include securing territory, nest building materials, access to the opposite gender, etc. Food related aggression is the dark side of appetitive behavior.

2.2.4.3. Escape vs Avoidance. The three main options in a painful or stressful situation are to retaliate aggressively, escape the situation, or avoid the situation. All three options are ways of protecting oneself from future harm. Animals that didn't escape or avoid harm were taken out of the gene pool.

2.2.4.3.1. Sometimes escaping the situation can take the form of **appeasement** or **submissive** behaviors. Many social species have innate behaviors to reduce aggression between animals. Dogs roll over on their backs.

2.2.4.3.2. **Avoidance behaviors** function to prevent, postpone, or delay the presentation (onset) of an aversive stimulus. Unconditioned avoidance behaviors may include hiding, detouring, or running away. A warning signal is the antecedent for an avoidance behavior. Many animals are trained to perform complex avoidance behaviors using the threat of an aversive stimulus.

2.2.4.3.3. **Counter-control** is the term for aggression an animal might use to get something it wants such as termination of an aversive stimulus or acquisition of an appetitive stimulus. It can range from mere non-compliance to physical aggression. It generally functions to get the animal more behavioral freedom when faced with aversive controlling attempts. If you have a little brother, you probably understand counter-control at a deep level.

2.2.4.4. **Emotional arousal** is an innate response to **appraisal** of change. The appraisal is based on the animal's experience and instincts. Training can modify the experience component that goes into the appraisal. It is only after the automatic neurochemical emotional response, that the animal may become aware of the resulting "feelings". The animal does not "decide" how to feel. Emotional arousal sets the stage for animals to make choices. If an aversive stimulus causes you to deviate from your path, you are less likely to experience significant emotional arousal if the aversive was a puddle, than if it was a hissing snake. Trainers want to be like puddles.

Zen behaviorist koan: What was the stimulus that caused you to answer this question? Ahh..Satori!

Chapter 11

3. Learning

Learning doesn't require reasoning; it's much faster than that!

3.1 Learning is a basic requirement of animal life. We are animals because we are able to learn. If we weren't, we would be plants. Plant trainers are few and far between.

3.2 Learning involves endogenous physical changes in the brain of the animal. The physical changes involve the creation of new and strengthening of existing connections between the nerve cells along which neurochemical signals pass. Unused connections wither away; the synapses are lost and neurons may actually die. It seems to be a pruning process, where the resouces are allocated to those parts of the system that are being used. So the more times the pathway is used by the traveling signal, the wider the pathway becomes. It's like a single track being worn into a super-highway. The signal speeds along the nerve cell itself as an electro-chemical wave and then makes the jump from cell to cell across the tiny gap between cells coded as a neurotranmitter.

Juvenile animals have many more neurons and connections than needed. Older animals have been through the neurological pruning process. An overwired, immature brain may have close to twice as many synapses as it will have as an adult. But an adult brain can be pushed into a period of synapse proliferation by putting the animal into a new, challenging environment. You *can* teach an old dog new tricks!

Training animals without an understanding of the processes involved can certainly be done, but the exciting 21st century unveiling of neurochemical processes gives us an opportunity to understand the training process at a much deeper level. Science is bringing forward new information about neurochemical processes every day. I think it is really exciting to realize that learning about neurochemistry could not only affect our own neurochemistry, but it could cause our brains to grow new connections. We live in a magical world!!

How 2 Train A _____

3.2 Types of Conditioning: The science of behavior gives us three very useful types of learning: Habituation, Respondent Conditioning, and Operant Conditioning

LEARNING	RULE	DESCRIPTION
Habituation	Stimulus alone – no contingency.	Decrease in response to stimulus due to exposure to the stimulus.
Respondent	New stimulus predicts old stimulus with total contingency..	Builds associations between stimuli to elicit involuntary responses.
Operant	Stimulus elicits response and consequences.	Consequences increase or decrease frequencies of learned behaviors.

Chapter 12

3.3 Habituation

3.3.1.1 **Habituation** is the decrease in an automatic response (usually an arousal or awareness) to a stimulus. Habituation occurs because the stimulus is presented repeatedly with no consequence attached. You quickly become habituated to the way your clothes feel or the ambient sounds in a room. Animal trainers sometimes use habituation by leaving stimuli in places where animals may be exposed to them.

The repeated presentation of the stimulus causes the neurons to reduce the amount of neurotransmitter dumped into the synapse, so the signal starts failing to migrate to the brain.

3.3.1.2 Sensitization, dishabituation, and desensitization are related to habituation.

3.3.1.2.1 The opposite of habituation is **sensitization**, which increases magnitude of response (including arousal or awareness principally). Sensitization involves attaching some significance to a neutral stimulus so it involves a greater degree of learning than mere exposure; for this reason sensitization generally comes under Respondent or Operant techniques. Sensitization involves increasing the amount of neurotransmitters sent across the neural synapse.

3.3.1.2.2 **Dishabituation** happens when the animal is finally getting used to some stimulus and there is a sudden event (usually a sound) that triggers an adrenaline response. Any habituation that had occurred is lost and the animal is more frightened of the original stimulus than when you started. The system is awash in neurotransmitters. Dishabituation is your enemy.

3.3.1.2.3 Training animals involves a great deal of desensitization and sensitization to different stimuli. **Desensitization** is not a type of habituation because it requires more complex learning than mere exposure. I address it here because they both relate to diminishing response to zero.

3.3.1.2.3.1 **Systematic desensitization** refers to a process involving respondent or operant conditioning to speed habituation. The process is graded exposure to incremental levels of stimulus intensity while maintaining relaxation in the animal. Relaxation inhibits a fear response. One of its uses is helping people who have phobias. Just relax now.... nothing to fear... just relax and close your eyes while I put this big spider in your lap. Oops!

Actually, if we were training you to accept spiders, we would start with a spider at a distance, allow you to see it and approach you until you showed any sign of vigilance. Then we would wait until you relaxed your vigilance and looked unconcerned, at which point we would quickly take the spider away. After 10 seconds or more, we would be back with our spider, slowly entering your zone of concern, then again waiting until you relaxed, before we scampered off with our spider. It might not even be conscious, but soon your brain would know the best way to get rid of that spider is to relax. Enough practice and your brain would associate spiders with relaxation. New spa concept? Doubtful, but this method is sometimes also called "approach and retreat".

Chapter 13

3.4 Respondent Conditioning

3.4.1 **Pavlovian** or **Classical** are other names for respondent learning. The term "classical" greatly confuses horse trainers because it implies long used techniques of European riding schools. It brings to mind (erroneously) 3-cornered velvet hats and Lipizzaner horses. No wonder the horse world is confused by contact with behaviorists! On the other hand, Pavlovian brings to mind (correctly) slobbering dogs. We will refer to it as "respondent".

3.4.2 **Respondent conditioning** always involves a reflexive automatic behavior such as blinking, shuddering, sneezing, or the innate processes of emotional arousal. Trainers are concerned with many reflexive behaviors such as the startle response and the opposition reflex (push against physical pressure). The response starts out "unconditioned", but then it gets a new stimulus attached to it, after which it is then called "conditioned". The response doesn't really change. It is still an innate behavior.

3.4.3 It is the stimulus that changes in respondent conditioning. For any reflexive behavior, there is a stimulus condition that naturally triggers the innate response. Respondent conditioning pairs the new and old stimuli to create a new trigger. To create an association by respondent conditioning, the new stimulus is presented just before (think milliseconds) the older known stimulus. In Pavlov's famous experiment, a bell was rung just before the dogs were fed, and soon the bell alone made the dogs salivate. The bell was the new stimulus, food was the old stimulus, and salivating was the innate response.

3.4.4 Respondent conditioning is the way organisms make associations between known stimuli and new ones. By pairing the known and new stimuli, the new one starts to function like the older one did. If the known stimulus elicited fear, the new one comes to elicit fear. These changes are not conscious processes that the animal can choose. The actions elicited, no matter whether they are emotional arousal or salivation, are things that are not voluntary. They evoke the response unconditionally. The animal never "decides" to be frightened any more than it "decides" to salivate.

3.4.4.1 Once a stimulus becomes a conditioned stimulus, it can then act as the known stimulus and be used to associate new pre-stimuli to the behavior. This is called **higher-order conditioning**. It doesn't seem to work after the 3rd iteration out from the unconditional stimulus.

3.4.4.2 If the new stimulus is something the animal is already familiar with, it will be more difficult to create the connection, a phenomenon known as **latent inhibition**.

3.4.5 If two pre-stimuli are presented at the same time, only one will be conditioned. This is called **overshadowing** and the most salient stimulus will prevent the other one from becoming conditioned. This could be in a sensory modality the trainer is not aware of (such as smell). This is a good reason to limit other sources of stimulation during respondent conditioning. Too many signals create confusion.

3.4.5.1 However, it is sometimes expedient to use overshadowing to prevent negative associations from being made. When necessity requires an aversive procedure, a disposable but highly salient stimulus can be used to minimize the damage to the trainer-animal relationship. This is called **blocking**.

3.4.5.2 If two pre-stimuli have a long history of being presented together before the conditioning, when one of them becomes a conditioned stimulus, the other will automatically have some conditioned effects.

3.4.6 If the association between stimuli is disrupted, the response to the conditioned stimulus, having no importance as a signal, will gradually weaken and be extinguished. This is **respondent extinction** and is discussed under Operant Conditioning: Absences of Consequences.

3.4.7 Timing is the most important aspect of respondent

conditioning. There are possible sequences of stimuli presentation with varying degrees of effectiveness.

- **Delay Procedure**. The best results occur when the pre-stimulus is presented first and the unconditional stimulus is presented before the pre-stimulus is terminated so that they overlap and co-terminate.
- **Backwards Procedure**. If the pre-stimulus is presented after the unconditional stimulus, no conditioning occurs.
- **Trace Procedure**. If the pre-stimulus is presented and terminated before the unconditional stimulus with a stimulus free period between them, conditioning will be inversely proportional to the length of the stimulus-free period, i.e. the closer the stronger.
- Delay between presentation of the pre-stimulus and unconditional stimulus of between 5-10 seconds best for autonomic responses, 0.4-1 second for musculature response.
- The vomiting response is a special case. Evolution has enabled quick learning to take place despite a long time between the stimulus and the response. Behaviorists gave this phenomenon a special name: "the **Garcia Effect**". Life-long food aversions can be acquired from a single event of food poisoning. You can also condition a taste aversion by feeding someone something and then taking them on a roller-coaster. File that under "experiments to try with Baby Brother".

3.4.8 The effectiveness of respondent conditioning can be maximized by attention to a few details.

- More repetitions of the pairing will increase the likelihood of correct response.
- The more strictly the "if-then" contingency is maintained, making the pre-stimulus totally predictive of the unconditional stimulus, the faster the animal will learn it. Total consistency of pairing, with no presentation of the pre-stimulus without the unconditional stimulus maintains its peak signal power, but the point of the training process is to eventually elicit the response using the conditioned signal instead of the unconditional

stimulus. It has to go on its own eventually.
- Adjust the intensity to make the pre-stimulus the most salient thing in the environment for the animal. Don't confuse things with extraneous noise or movements.
- Be realistic about your individual animal's capabilities, taking the time it takes to get the results you want. You will get better respondent conditioning results with animals and humans that are more excitable and it will be more difficult with the sedate ones. Animal trainers aren't surprised when the calm ones are a little bit harder to train.
- Some stimulus modalities may be hard to connect with some modes of response. Trainers typically use tactile, auditory, or visual signals. Taste or smells are more difficult to work with.

3.4.9 Respondent conditioning is the cause of many "irrational" emotions. Truly neutral stimuli get accidentally associated with emotional arousal such as fear. Avoidance can prevent exposure that might extinguish the response. A French study of equine fear used white shirts as the fear-producing stimulus. Apparently French veterinarians all wear white shirts and so French horses are fearful of people in white shirts. No, I am *not* making this up. It was in a scientific journal!

3.4.10 Counter-conditioning. or perception-modification, involves teaching the animal to have a pleasant feeling and reaction toward something that it once feared or disliked. This procedure supplies a way to eliminate a classically conditioned response. The conditioned stimulus that the animal is fearful of is paired with an unconditioned stimulus for a response that is stronger than the conditioned response and which cannot occur at the same time as the conditioned response. Usually this means making the conditioned stimulus predict arrival of food. We talked about using it to connect spiders and relaxation in the last chapter.

3.4.10.1 Use this strategy with a plan for systematic desensitization to deal with really tough situations. Associate the fear stimulus with food by presenting the fear stimulus at a distance during repetitions of food delivery. When that association is made, require the animal to exhibit relaxation as a signal for you to present the fear stimulus which has become a signal that the food is arriving. When the animal relaxes, the stimulus signals impending reward. Then the stimulus can be brought gradually into the proximity of the animal.

3.4.10.2 When a problem behavior involves strong emotional arousal (i.e. fear), it is very useful to leave operant conditioning until later and focus on changing the emotions using respondent conditioning. Bob Bailey calls this "having Pavlov get bigger on your shoulder".

Chapter 14

3.5 Operant Conditioning

3.5.1 The Law of Effect was codified around the turn of the 20th century by E.L. Thorndike. It recognized that behaviors were influenced by "trial and error" activities that would speed learning through favorable or "annoying" consequences.
The **Law of Effect** says that behaviors that produce valued outcomes are repeated while behaviors that produce aversive outcomes are modified or suppressed. From the time of the ancient Greeks, people had known that pleasure and pain motivated behaviors, but Thorndike approached the issue with the tools of science: empirical evidence and sound measurement. Armed with a stopwatch, he put cats in boxes and watched them figure out how to escape.

3.5.2 Working from where Thorndike left off, B.F. Skinner continued investigating the causes of behavior. In 1938, Skinner published a book on the principles of what he called "**operant conditioning**". He is the guy that raised his baby daughter in a operant conditioning chamber and she turned out fine.

3.5.3 **Operant behaviors** "operate" on the environment. The organism is doing something to control its world. The change that occurs in the animal's world is a consequence of its behavior. Notice the contrast with respondent behaviors, which were instinctive and involuntary.

3.5.4 Consequences increase or decrease the likelihood of a behavior being repeated. If the consequences are unpleasant, the behavior will be less likely to be repeated; but if the consequence is pleasant the behavior is more likely to be repeated. Your job as a trainer is to control the consequences.

3.5.5 Operant behaviors involve voluntary behaviors and choice. Choice, defined in this paradigm, is where there are alternative ways to obtain reinforcement (but not necessarily the same reinforcement for alternative behaviors). You could choose to go to work or to go to the beach. The consequences would be different.

3.5.6 The contingency statement

3.5.7 Let's review that all important Contingency Statement. It is about to get really important:

Antecedents -> Behaviors -> Consequences

Chapter 15

3.5.6 Antecedents

Because behavior is an unending flow, interrupted only by death, antecedents also constitute a flowing phenomenon, one superseding the last as time goes forward. A zillion factors are integrated into the reasons for any particular behavior, but we can tease them apart conceptually and put them into categories of triggers for the behavior.

3.5.6.1 **Phylogenetic History** sets the stage. The animal brings a genetic inheritance to the table. Its ancestors whose behavior became sensitive to biologically important events likely survived and reproduced to pass the propensity to respond to subsequent generations. The animal before you contains the story of what worked for its ancestors. Nature has prepared the horse to walk onto the diving board, but not to enter the water. The dolphin is going to have a problem with that diving board.

3.5.6.2 **History of Reinforcement** pops out as a very important factor when you start comparing learning rates of individual animals. An empowered animal has been reinforced for finding a solution to its challenges.

3.5.6.2.1 **Positive and Negative Transfer**: Past learning can help or hinder new learning. Thorndike and his associates explored how individuals would transfer learning in one context to another context that shared similar characteristics. He examined the question of whether learning in one context, helps problem solving in another context. He was the guy that proved that Latin or Greek might not be important elements of a basic education. His graphs and test scores changed our world!

3.5.6.2.2 **Learning Sets**: The rate of learning to solve new problems improves through practice of solving similar problems. Animals (including humans) learn to learn. They learn general rules for problem solving and then can apply them to solve a new problem. Some species can understand more complex rules, while some are limited to very simple rules. Managing the learning set is an advanced skill for animal trainers.

3.5.6.3 Current conditions are the antecedents we are most likely to notice and those most immediately under our control.

3.5.6.3.1 The physiological state of the animal is critical. If it is sick, it cannot function. For best results insure that your animal is in optimum health. Consider everything: medical problems, diet; pain; parasites; teeth/beak health, indigestion; hormonal states, adequacy of exercise, and mental stimulation. Physiological problems cause neurochemistry consequences. The neurochemistry of the animal can't be optimal for learning if it's body is responding to physical stress.

3.5.6.3.2 Motivation is critical. **Motivating Operations** are done to alter the appetitiveness or aversiveness of the stimulus. For positive reinforcement training, the timing of food delivery is managed to enhance appetitiveness of food reward (but if the animal is too hungry, it won't learn much). Introduction of an aversive stimulus is a motivating operation for negative reinforcement. The Food Management Plan is discussed under Environmental Management in Chapter 22.1.

3.5.6.3.3 **Concurrent Contingencies** create distraction. There are always other stimuli impacting the behavior of the animal at any one time. Competition between contingencies experienced by the animal will reduce training effectiveness. Competition between contingencies experienced by the trainer is probably even more fatal to the training session, unless it is a "cell phone moment" in a negative reinforcement session. More on that in Chapter 22 .

3.5.6.3.4 Presentation of the stimulus for the behavior is the final piece of the antecedent conditions. **Stimulus control** is the measure of how reliably the animal will perform the behavior in response to the presentation of the cue. Some trainers consider stimulus control to be all or nothing. For my personal style, 100% reliability is a utopian goal.

To summarize this chapter with a bottom line: Control of the antecedent environment is one of the two most important training tools in any trainers tool box.

Chapter 16

3.5.8 Behaviors

3.5.8.1 Few behaviors will be learned in their final form. Most go through stages of polishing. The following list is a general sequence that all trained behaviors go through. Any behavior can be rated from 1 to 5, but if it doesn't respond to the cue immediately it can have a rating of no more than two. Some animals go from one to four in just a few minutes.

1. **Basic Attempt**: this is the rough try when you start out.
2. **Obedience**: immediate response to the cue.
3. **Self-Maintenance**: the animal stays on task until released.
4. **Relaxed Engagement**: the animal performs with visible confidence.
5. **Reliable**: the animal performs anywhere, under any circumstance.

3.5.8.2 Behaviors have qualities that can be strengthened by reinforcement. Once the animal has a basic attempt on cue, the trainer can focus on improving each of these qualities (but only one at a time and in this order).

- **Frequency**: In the beginning you just need to increase the frequency of the crudely correct behavior. This will put the basic attempt on cue.
- **Latency**: When the animal will consistently perform the behavior, you can modify the criteria for reinforcement to be within a certain amount of time. With positive reinforcement, this looks like a time limited offer; if the animal does not respond within the time set, the offer expires. When using negative reinforcement, the usual practice is to sequentially increase the aversive nature of the stimulus, creating a window of time for an avoidance response. Don't make the window so short that it is not possible for the animal to physically perform the behavior in the time given. Help your animal succeed. You create obedience by shortening latency.

- **Duration**: When the animal will obediently perform the correct behavior, it is time to ask for the animal to stay on task until released. It is unwise to train duration before you have the final desired form of the behavior because they think they are supposed to patiently wait. Don't ask me how I know this. You create self-maintenance by lengthening duration.
- **Engagement**: You can increase engagement by reinforcing qualities such as amplitude, energy, posture, etc. This will vary widely for each type of behavior. The result should be relaxed, confident engagement.
- **Location**: You can save location until you have a otherwise finished behavior, or you can broaden location from the beginning. I like to "dare" them to perform in all kinds of places.
- **With Distraction**: When the behavior becomes a habitual response to the cue, reliability becomes truly possible.

3.5.8.3 Shaping

3.5.8.3.1 Some behaviors are too complex to learn immediately or occur so infrequently they can't be captured. The method to get these behaviors is **successive approximation**. This involves using a graduated series of small improvements towards a goal. Using shaping, the trainer, can modify crude responses into incredible behaviors no one suspected the animal could perform. The criterion for reinforcement is gradually shifted from one approximation to the next, until the **target behavior** is performed. The key is to know exactly what you are trying to get and then to reinforce any change in that direction. If the animal is allowed to practice an approximation too many times (that would be about 7), then it may get stuck and not want to move to the next approximation. In general, if the animal is successful three times in a row with one approximation, it is time to move to the next. (Other trainers use an 80% rule, shifting criteria when the animal performs well 80% of the time.) The changes between approximations should be very small in any case.

3.5.8.3.2 Shaping can take place using prompts to guide

the animal or it can capitalize on the spontaneous variation produced at the beginning of extinction. Many trainers feel that shaping without prompts creates a more "empowered" animal, displaying more persistence and creativity. The procedure without prompts is called **Free Shaping**. It might be called "free", but animal trainers know it takes extra time and attention to details.

Teaching the animal to touch a specific part of its body to an object is called **targetting**, with the object, which might be the trainer's hand, being the **target**. Targetting can greatly speed the shaping of a behavior.

3.5.8.3.3 **Capturing** a behavior is, in some ways, the opposite of shaping a behavior. In capturing it, you reinforce the animal whenever it spontaneously offers the behavior. Then when the frequency of the behavior has been increased, you put it on cue, by associating availability of reinforcement with the cue stimulus. The trick is catching the animal in the act. I taught my dog to sneeze on cue by reinforcing her random sneezes. We were doing a lot of traveling and it was convenient to catch her in the act as she sat on the car seat next to me. Even so, it took several months to get stimulus control.

3.5.8.4 **Chains**

3.5.8.4.1 Behavior chains are made of sequences of individual behaviors that must be performed in a specific order to earn reinforcement. Only the terminal behavior is overtly reinforced. Three types are: forward chaining, backward chaining, and total task presentation.

3.5.8.4.1.1 **Task Analysis**, making a written plan, is the first step. The entire chain must be broken into its component parts ("links") with a description of each link in order. If a video of the behavior chain exists, it is invaluable to study it in detail, paying careful attention to the transitions between the links. It also will help to validate the plan by pretending to be the animal and seeing what it feels like to go from link to link. There is no penalty to erasing and starting over when you are doing it on paper. It is hard to change when the animal has already learned some of it.

3.5.8.4.1.2 The most efficient way to link behaviors in general is starting with the last one in the series. This is called **backward chaining**. The last behavior (the one you start with) is always reinforced. Then each link is added in reverse sequential order. The last behavior to be added is the one that the behavior chain starts with.

3.5.8.4.1.2.1 This works well because the final behaviors end up with the strongest history of reinforcement. The opportunity to perform them becomes reinforcing. The **Premack Principle** says that behaviors with a stronger history of reinforcement can become the reinforcement for other behaviors. This principle is a excellent tool for training.

It is also a pitfall trap for the unsuspecting trainer who tries to stop unwanted behaviors by redirecting the animal to a familiar behavior. Sophisticated trainers know redirecting will reinforce what the animal is doing at the moment of redirection.

3.5.8.4.1.2.2 Independently learned and reinforced behaviors can be connected if backward chaining is not convenient for some reason. They can be connected in any kind of subsets, or added one by one.

3.5.8.4.1.2.3 Training a chain in a forwards direction is harder because the animal gets frustrated when it completed one behavior and now has to try to guess what to do next.

3.5.8.5 **Targeting** and **Stationing** are two very useful behaviors.

3.5.8.5.1 Targeting is touching an object with a body part. Targeting is extremely useful for many applications, allowing the animal to be directed without restraint. If animals are taught to target two parts of their body at the same time, they can be put into almost any position or place.

3.5.8.5.2 Stationing is staying on a predefined place for some duration. Stationing makes it possible to work with multiple animals and it creates a place where you can put the animal if you need to do something in its cage, etc. Putting the station in a place the animal prefers to be makes it easier to get the animal to stay there. The station itself will be more useful if it is movable.

3.5.8.6 Superstitious behaviors are ones mistakenly included in a contingency relationship. They might be maintained indirectly by the variables that control another behavior, rather than directly by their own typical controlling variables or they might persist in the intervals between reinforcements for another behavior. Animal trainers are prone to superstitious behaviors too.... especially about hats!

Chapter 17

3.5.9 Consequences

3.5.9.1 As feedback influencing future behavior, consequences can increase or decrease the likelihood that the preceding behavior will be repeated. Note that they don't actually change the single instance of a behavior but just influence the probability of it happening again.

3.5.9.2 Qualities of Effective Consequences

3.5.9.2.1 **Contiguous**. The extent to which events occur close together in time and/or location strongly affects the animal's ability to recognize associations. Less than 1 second is contiguous, and 10 seconds or more might as well be never. Animals need immediate feedback.

3.5.9.2.2 **Contingent**. If the consequence is delivered consistently and therefore totally predictable, the animal will not be confused by the rules varying from moment to moment and will learn faster.

3.5.9.2.3 Value. The **Matching Law** says that the relative rates of different behaviors tend to match the relative rates of reinforcement they produce. There is a whole science of Behavioral Economics that studies the question of value on choice making. The operant chamber with its lever-pressing rats has been used as a way to study microeconomics and consumer choice. Most of the literature of this exciting field includes differential equations and mathematical problems like Lever A producing 80% of the reinforcement while Lever B produces 20%. Which will the animal choose 80% of the time? What if Lever B gives carrots and Lever A gives lumps of coal? Oh dear! In a statistical way, the response rates will track the reinforcement rates. The bottom line for trainers is that higher value reinforcers delivered more frequently result in more effort expended to get them. Nothing too mathematically precise, just a vague guideline: small and higher value are more motivating.

3.5.9.3 Consequences increase or decrease the frequency of behavior.

3.5.9.3.1 Consequences are what the quadrants of the behavior model are really all about. The same material is in each of the three following charts. Study them carefully.

Let's pretend we are mad (but not really mean or angry) scientists for a moment and we have put a tiny wire into our animal subjects brain. If we push the APPETITIVE button, the animal suddenly gets a very pleasurable sensation. If we push the AVERSIVE button, the animal gets a very annoying buzz in its head. We can only use one button per animal and we have a very specific rule for when to push it or when to stop pushing it. The rule is "when the animal lifts its right foot off the ground".

	Appetitive Stimuli	Aversive Stimuli
Present stimulus in response to behavior	Increases Behavior	Decreases Behavior
Remove stimulus in response to behavior	Decreases Behavior	Increases Behavior

Using the table and narrative above, figure out the answer to these questions. The answers are at the end of this chapter.

A. What 2 ways can you use your buttons to train the animal to keep its foot in the air?

B. What 2 ways can you use your buttons to train the animal to never lift its foot off the ground?

Grab a business-card-sized piece of paper and cover the next chart before you examine it. Slide your paper so you can see the top row and the row on the left side. Now guess which the four covered boxes say "present stimulus" and which say "remove stimulus".

	Increase Behavior	Decrease Behavior
Appetitive stimuli	Present stimulus in response to behavior	Remove stimulus in response to behavior
Aversive stimuli	Remove stimulus in response to behavior	Present stimulus in response to behavior

Now we just have to attach a couple of terms. If you increase the behavior, it is **reinforcement**. If you decrease the behavior, it is **punishment**. If you present a stimulus it is **positive**. If you remove a stimulus, it is **negative**.

Cover the next chart as before and apply the correct terms: 1) positive or negative, 2) reinforcement or punishment, and 3) state what kind of stimulus you need to do it.

	Increase Behavior	Decrease Behavior
Present Stimulus in response to behavior	Positive Reinforcement using appetitive stimulus	Positive Punishment using aversive stimulus
Remove Stimulus in response to behavior	Negative Reinforcement using aversive stimulus	Negative Punishment using appetitive stimulus

Okay, Mad Scientist, the fun is over, put that poor animal away, because we have to get back to the lecture.

3.5.9.4 Absence of Consequences: **Extinction**

3.5.9.4.1 Extinction is a reduction in frequency of behavior as a result of the disassociation between the behavior and access to reinforcement. When the probability of finding reinforcement is zero, the probability of the behavior will go to zero. How long will you keep going to your job if they quit paying you?

3.5.9.4.2 **Response induction** is the first sign extinction is underway. At the initiation of the extinction procedure, the rate of behavior will increase (**extinction burst**) and new behaviors will be offered to try to access the reinforcement. The new behavior might be aggression towards the trainer! The Animal Trainer expects things to get a little bit crazy before things settle down.

3.5.9.4.3 Extinction is the conceptually simplest, most direct method of reducing the frequency of a behavior and it plays prominent role in stimulus discrimination training. Other methods of reducing the frequency are discussed in Section 5 of this chapter under Punishment. Extinction works best when the reinforcement for the behavior is under complete control.

3.5.9.4.3.1 There is a special name for a conditioned stimulus that is slated for extinction: **S-Delta** or SΔ. In normal English, they call it a "discriminative stimuli for extinction", but most trainers only know it as S-Delta. Then, after it no longer evokes a response it is back to just being a "neutral stimulus".

3.5.9.4.3.2 Of course, innate responses to unconditional stimuli cannot be extinguished. Only learned associations can be dismantled.

3.5.9.4.4 Extinction of escape or avoidance behaviors has two rules: 1) if the behavior is not in process, present the stimulus in the least intrusive way possible (at a distance) and remove it when the animal is relaxed; and 2) if the behavior is in process, do not terminate the stimulus until the animal is not reacting to it. Rule 2 is problematic in that it causes emotional arousal in both the animal and the trainer. Skillful application of Rule 1 is preferred in all cases.

3.5.9.4.4.1 Response prevention measures may speed the process. If the behavior is hard to execute, it will be less likely to occur.

3.5.9.4.4.2 To speed the process even more, provide an alternate way the animal can access the reinforcement it was receiving from performing the behavior. If possible provide that reinforcement in excess.

3.5.9.4.4.3 Application of Rule 2 with a high intensity stimulus is called **flooding**, or "sacking out" in the horse world. Practitioners of this method confine their animal to prevent escape behaviors from being performed, and then apply the stimulus until the animal stops responding to it. This method is quite controversial because of the emotional arousal issues, the likelihood of the appraisal of the stimulus being transferred to the trainer, and because it generally reflects a crude understanding and application of the laws. It kind of works, but using Rule 1, shows more finesse.

3.5.9.4.5 The problems associated with extinction are that 1) the reinforcement currently maintaining the unwanted behavior may be difficult to identify or eliminate; 2) it is slow; there are potential side effects; and 3) it does not establish alternative behavior to access the reinforcement gained by the unwanted behavior.

3.5.9.4.5.1 The response merely diminishes over time (think downward curve not cliff).

3.5.9.4.5.2 Spontaneous recovery of the extinguished response can be set off by a single instance of reinforced behavior. Then there will be all of that response induction to live through again. Sigh....

3.5.9.4.5.3 **Disinhibition** is the temporary increase in the frequency of an extinguished response caused by an unrelated stimulus event. It is important to prevent reinforcement of these occurrences to prevent spontaneous recovery.

3.5.9.4.6 The "will to try" can be extinguished. **Learned Helplessness** is a condition that results from exposure to inescapable aversive stimulation. Many trainers call it "shut down". The animal can't even try. It may create a false sense that the animal is calmly accepting its servitude, but there will be no joy in it. Training new behaviors to an animal with learned helplessness is very difficult. To remedy the situation, the animal must be convinced that it has some control over its world. This requires a dedicated and compassionate trainer.

How 2 Train A _____   69

3.6 Respondent and the various types of Operant Conditioning are not really separable in practice.

3.6.1 You can never interact with the animal without yourself and your cues becoming an emotional stimulus. Good or bad, it is going to affect your relationship. If the balance is on the good side, the animal is going to forgive you more often. (You are naive if you think that doesn't matter.)

3.6.2 Respondent behaviors can be modified to a certain extent with operant conditioning. We previously discussed systematic desensitization under respondent conditioning. It combines the operant behavior relaxing with appraisal of and habituation to a stimulus. Controlling autonomic body functions with operant conditioning, like shaping brain wave state changes, are direct applications of mixing of the two types of conditioning.

3.6.3 When extinction is used to weaken some behavior and reinforcement is used to instill a behavior to replace it, it is called **Differential Reinforcement**. This will be discussed in the Alternatives to Punishment section.

3.6.4 Some behaviors result in mixed reinforcing and punishing consequences. Training theory provides a way to predict the result. At first the behavior frequency may be decreased, but if the punishers are only moderate, the behavior often "recovers" to a level equal to that seen with only the reinforcers. Then if the punishing stimulus ceases, however, there may be a "burst" (overshoot) of responding, demonstrating that the responding was suppressed to some extent. The importance of this topic is that none of these processes happen in isolation

----------------------ANSWERS--------------------
A. Keep the foot in the air by using the rule with: 1) APPETITIVE button, push it when animal lifts foot, or 2) AVERSIVE button, stop pushing it whenever animal lifts his foot.

B. Keep the foot on the ground using the rule with: 1) AVERSIVE button, push it when animal lifts foot; or 2) APPETITIVE button, stop pushing it whenever animal lifts his foot.

Chapter 18

4. Reinforcement: it increases behaviors

Given a choice, all creatures tend to do the things that are most rewarding to them.

4.1 **Stimulus Control** is when the behavior will be performed in response to one stimulus but not in response to any other other stimuli. It is generally gained by pairing the specific cue consistently with reinforcement and putting the behavior on an extinction schedule in the absence of the cue. It helps to use two very different cues to clarify to the animal when you are requesting a performance (presenting the SD) as opposed to indicating that no reinforcement is available at this time (presenting the SΔ). It also helps the animal focus on the cue if the amount of time the cue will be presented is unpredictable to the animal. The cues can be diminished or changed after the behavior is reliably on cue. The outcome of stimulus control is a particular behavior will be automatically performed in response to the presentation of the cue. When you can add, "under all circumstances", you know the behavior is under total stimulus control.

4.1.1 There is something called an **Errorless Discrimination** procedure that can be used to help the animal's ability to discriminate between stimuli. This involves helping the animal detect the difference between the stimuli without offering the opportunity for error. The SΔ signaled periods are kept short to begin with and slowly increased. The animal may be restrained (leashed) so that performance of the behavior is not possible during the SΔ signaled period. The advantage of using Errorless Discrimination procedures is that it does not create frustration for the animal. The disadvantage is that it is hard to make changes to these strongly conditioned cues. That might be a problem if the animal changes owners or trainers. Sometimes it is best for things to be a little sloppy.

4.2 Positive Reinforcement

4.2.1 **Bridges** connect moments of time to reinforcement delivery. They start out as a cue to start feeding-related behaviors, and eventually they become an event marker to tag the moment when the behavior requested was performed.

4.2.1.1 To establish the bridge as a conditioned reinforcer, pair it with an established food reinforcer, presenting the bridge milliseconds prior to presentation of the reinforcer. After a few dozen presentations the animal will show anticipation of receiving the food when the bridge is presented. Until the animal has a good history of the bridge signaling positive consequences, keep the behaviors very simple and minimize any delay between the bridge and food delivery.

4.2.1.2 Not just a clicker! Bridges can be made from auditory, tactile or visual neutral stimulus. Animals can learn to respond to a variety of bridges. Whistles and clickers are popular commercially available products, but the human voice seems to work every bit as well. The bridge should be very salient against the background of stimuli impinging on the animal.

Tactile bridges (touches, taps, or scratches) are extremely useful when training multiple animals.

4.2.1.3 Do not use your bridge for ANYTHING else. It should convey a very specific meaning to the animal.

4.2.1.4 There is a great deal of controversy about the consequences of clicking and not following it with a reward. If the stimulus is not totally contingent with the outcome, there will be a loss of predictive value to the animal. If 50% or more of the signals are not followed with reward, the signal is of no predictive value. We recommend that you avoid presenting the bridge for any one instance if in doubt, but that if you bridged it, you have an obligation to reward for it, unless the animal breaks the social contract with an aggressive behavior between bridging and delivery. More on this hot topic in Chapter 22

4.2.2 **Reinforcers**

4.2.2.1 Choosing good ones is important.

4.2.2.1.1 Reinforcers are relative to the current environment and what the animal requires to maintain homeostasis.

4.2.2.1.2 **Primary reinforcers**: food, social interaction, physical activity, control, sensory experience, and escape from aversives. These do not depend on a history of reinforcement to be reinforcing.

4.2.2.1.3 **Secondary reinforcers**: ANYTHING that has a strong history of being paired with a primary reinforcer.

4.2.2.1.4 Factors that affect the efficacy of reinforcement: type, frequency, magnitude, intensity, duration, availability, novelty, and variety.

4.2.2.1.5 Small frequent reinforcers are more effective than big occasional reinforcers.

4.2.2.1.6 A higher frequency behavior can be used to reinforce a lower frequency behavior: this is called the **Premack Principle**.

4.2.2.1.7 The SD becomes reinforcing over time, the animals seem to enjoy competence, and certainly enjoy the ability to control the environment.

4.2.2.2 Temporal Aspects of Delivery. Delay between the behavior and the reinforcement results in a discounting of reinforcer effectiveness. The quicker the delivery, the faster the behavior frequency will increase. "Ho Hum… oh, the treat?, oh, .. yeah!… it's still in my pocket.. here you go, little buddy. Thanks for being so patient." This rule can be exploited both ways by a savvy animal trainer.

4.2.2.3 The Matching Law: Effort = Reward Value

4.2.2.3.1 The Matching Law explains why so many lottery tickets are sold when the prizes get big.

4.2.2.3.2 If possible, increase your reinforcement rate in the middle of a training session and notice what happens. There should be a quick change in motivation. If there is no change, something might be inhibiting your animal from performing as well as it could. If suddenly you get an overwhelming amount of change, you may be being too stingy normally. If you are already feeding at maximum, then it isn't possible.

4.2.2.3.3 Reinforcer effectiveness changes with experience and is relative to what the animal is expecting. If it gets more value than what is expected, there is a positive **contrast**. If it gets less value than expected, the contrast is negative. Animals seem to understand and resent stinginess.

4.2.2.3.4 Anticipatory **contrast** is developed by conditioning a signal that a better than normal reinforcement is available. It can be used to occasionally motivate extra energy, extra precision, or extra quickness. It cannot be used all the time or it becomes the expected level of reinforcement. Favorite foods are good for developing anticipatory contrast. We have a protocol named Five-Bites that helps to overcome challenging tasks.

4.2.3 **Schedules** dictate which incidence of behavior will be reinforced.

4.2.3.1 Continuous Schedule. Each occurrence of the behavior is reinforced. This schedule is useful at the beginning of training, but the behaviors on this schedule are most susceptible to extinction when reinforcement is not available. A change from continuous schedule of reinforcement sometimes results in extinction-induced aggression when the animal is trying to figure out how to get the food that is suddenly no longer offered.

4.2.3.2 Some behaviorist, perhaps Skinner himself, got tired of having to get so many reinforcements ready and started investigating the effect of skipping treats. An intermittent (or partial) schedule specifies that there is only a probability of reinforcement for any particular instance of behavior. The probability might relate to the time passed since the last reinforcement or the number of behaviors performed since the last reinforcement. Skipping treats by an intermittent schedule of reinforcement builds in resistance to extinction because the animal has learned to expect periods of no reinforcement. Each type of schedule results in a particular rate of response in a statistical way.

EFFECT OF SCHEDULE ON RATE OF RESPONSE

	Intervals (amount of time)	Ratios (number of behaviors)
Fixed (Consistent)	Low rate of behavior at the start of the interval and high rate as the time for reinforcement approaches	High rate of behavior and with a pause after each reinforcement
Intermittent (Variable)	Moderate rate of behavior.	High rate of behavior.

4.2.3.2.1 Examples of the probability of reinforcement for any one behavior. Figure out why the probabilities are as stated.

SCHEDULE OF REINFORCEMENT	PROBABILITY OF REINFORCEMENT
Continous	100% probability for each response
Fixed Ratio of 2 responses per treat	Probability for 1st response is 0%, but probability for second response is 100%
Fixed Interval of 1 minute	Probability is 0% until the minute is over, then the probability for the next one is 100%
Variable Ratio averaging 2 responses	Probability for the 1st response is 50%, probability for the 2nd response is 50%
Variable Interval averaging 1 minute	The probability of reinforcement increases as time goes by.

4.4 Negative Reinforcement

4.4.1 Negative reinforcement combined with habituation is the typical style of training your dog on a leash or your horse on a leadline. This style is often called Compulsion Training because it basically forces them to comply. This doesn't mean it is necessarily violent. In the horse world, it is called pressure / release training and it forms the basis of Natural Horsemanship.

4.4.2 **Negative reinforcement** works because the animal is instinctively driven to resolve physical or psychological discomfort. They seek some way to find comfort and when they find the action that results in relief, they remember it and are more likely to try it the next time that problem surfaces.

4.4.3 Whatever response the animal has exhibited immediately prior to the release of aversive pressure is the one he remembers and associates as the way to escape that pressure. This technique requires good timing.

4.4.4 It also requires a pre-existing aversive, and the moment that the aversive stimulus is introduced can be experienced as a punishment for whatever the animal was doing at the time. Delicacy is required. Animal Trainers don't start annoying their animals when the animals are trying to please them.

4.4.5 **Escape Conditioning** is operant conditioning in which the behavior is reinforced because it causes a negative event to cease (a form of negative reinforcement). Escape conditioning is learned fast and is committed to memory quickly. Animals are prewired to avoid having to practice escape.

4.4.5.1 Escape behaviors can be shaped. If the stimulus is kept very minimally threatening and terminated at the first hint of the desired behavior, the animal will learn to control the stimulus. For many unhandled animals, merely having the trainer's attention or body turned toward the animal is sufficiently aversive to be a useful training tool.

4.4.5.2 If the aversive stimulation is too intense, emotional arousal will interfere with training.

4.4.5.3 The animal may learn to ignore the stimulus. Having a variety of low level aversives or handling the aversive in a way that seems unpredictable to the animal will extend the life of a low level aversive, but ultimately it is necessary to either increase the stimulus for escape (not a desirable option) or train for avoidance.

4.4.5.4 Some compulsion trainers use rapid escalation of pressure - it doesn't give the animal time to habituate to ineffective pressure. This procedure is not recommended.

4.4.6 **Avoidance Conditioning** is operant conditioning in which the behavior is reinforced, because it prevents something undesirable from happening (the other form of negative reinforcement). Avoidance conditioning is much less likely to arouse problematic emotions. Because avoidance prevents contact with the aversive, the animal does not become habituated to the aversive.

4.4.6.1 **Signaled avoidance** or **discriminative avoidance**. In the operant chamber the light comes on and the rat has 3 seconds to press the lever before the floor becomes electrified. The rat will get extremely good at this job, but it has to have been trained to press the lever to terminate the shock first.

4.4.6.2 Before presenting the aversive stimulus, a non-aversive discriminative stimulus is presented. The discriminative stimulus should be specific for one behavior. Trainers who use it, often consider it to be the equivalent of saying "Please". This Please signal should precede the aversive stimulus (the "Do it" signal) by sufficient time for the animal to start to respond (at least a second) and if the animal has started to respond the aversive is not presented. Marking the correct behavior with a unique negative reinforcement bridge signal can foster the development of that bridge functioning as a safety signal.

4.4.6.3 Presentation of the "Please" signal can start from the beginning when the behavior is being shaped. It can also then become the "reason" that aversive stimulus is presented, making it less likely that the onset of the aversive functions as a punishment for desirable behaviors.

4.4.7 The results of good negative reinforcement training are more reliable under stress than positive reinforcement. This is something horse riders appreciate.

4.4.8 Problems of Compulsion: no one likes it. Period. Wait... modify that.... masochists like it. For everyone else it is annoying by definition. It generates negative emotional arousal. It creates adversarial relationships. It fosters escape behaviors. Your animal will want to avoid you.

4.4.9 Imagine for a moment that you are walking down a path and you see something you have to detour around... puddle (emotional arousal factor 1) or SNAKE!!! (emotional arousal factor 10). These both generate the same avoidance behavior.

4.4.10 Control eventually can become positive. As the animal becomes practiced in this avoidance response, vigilance for the conditioned stimuli replaces fear and the stimuli become less aversive. Puddle jumping, anyone?

Chapter 19

Cowboy Interlude:

A translation of Ray Hunt into Applied Animal Behavior Analysis. Selected quotations from "Think Harmony with Horses: an in-depth study of Horse/Man Relationship" by Ray Hunt. 1978.

Ray Hunt was the most influential American in the so called "Revolution in Horsemanship" which is a method based on negative reinforcement and known by the name of Natural Horsemanship. The Natural Horsemanship trainers are masters of the use of negative reinforcement. Other animal trainers would do well to study them.

> "The ideas sound simple and they are easy to understand but they are the hardest thing in the world to apply because they involve handling ourselves as we handle the horse."
> Jesse Lair, reviewing Think Harmony with Horses.

[The horse is]... "an individual and that is why I say he's entitled to his thoughts just as you are entitled to yours."	Each animal brings its own history of reinforcement to the corral.
"Admire the horse for the good things he does and just kind of ignore the wrong things. First thing you know, the good things will get better and the bad things will get less."	Reinforce the desirable behaviors and the animal will have less time to engage in behaviors that don't gain access to a reinforcer.

"Don't make the horse do all the work. He shouldn't have to figure you out and learn to get out of your way to get things done."	It is the trainer's responsibility to set up the antecedent conditions.
"But you have to work to understand him, understand his problem, understand his qualities, whether you think they are good or bad or whatever. They are all good. So you don't try to change anything with the horse – you just build on."	Don't look at your horse's behavior as a pathological condition, instead look at what he needs to learn.
"Don't be afraid to expose your horse to something he hasn't quite been exposed to yet, but don't snow him under."	Introduce new stimuli in a way that minimizes their intensity.
"Don't be afraid to overemphasize or exaggerate a movement when you are trying to let your idea become the horse's idea."	Make your cues extremely salient to begin with.
"He makes decisions. If we're not there to help him, he may make a decision we don't want to make. Then we blame it on the horse. But, I grant you, it's not the horses fault."	The animal lives in a flow of behaviors and antecedent conditions, if we are not managing the antecedents, something undesirable (from our perspective) may become more salient to the animal.

"He will have learned it because you have offered it in an understanding way. You've made it enjoyable for your horse to learn. You've worked on the level he understands. You've kept his mind right and let him know ahead of time what you wanted so he doesn't have to become bothered."	Emotional arousal can be avoided by careful training, providing plenty of reinforcement, working from what the animal already knows, and building strong signaled avoidance behaviors from minimally aversive stimulation.
"If I had to work for you and I could do your thing my way and like it, this would benefit us both. But, if I had to do your thing your way and I didn't like it, it just wouldn't be me; you'd be wrong in expecting me to stay and I'd be wrong in staying."	If you are training with compulsion, then escape and avoidance behaviors are to be expected.
"If you are going to teach a horse something and have a good relationship, you don't make him learn it – you let him learn it."	If you arrange antecedent conditions in such a way as to invite him to the behavior that terminates the aversive, you can avoid becoming associated with the aversive stimulus.
"If you haven't got his attention you don't try to direct it."	If motivation is lacking for any reason, reinforcement is not going to work, and persisting in training will lead to unwanted results. Analyze drops in motivation and change the antecedent conditions. Might be time to quit.

"If you're going to head anything off, or get things into really coming along fast, you have to be aware of the indications the horse gives out."	Training is the "study of one" and the training plan needs to be constantly adapted to the current conditions.
"The horse learns not to be particular if the rider is not particular."	The horse will discriminate or generalize according to what it is conditioned to do
"Respect is understanding, not fear."	Fear is an emotional arousal that is always a problem. No type of training profits from it.
"It takes some physical pressure naturally, to start with, but you keep doing less and less physical and more and more mental. Pretty soon it's just a feel following a feel, whether it comes today, tomorrow, or next year."	Using signaled avoidance and then fading the discriminative stimulus will make the performance seem totally willing.
"Let the horse teach you what to do."	Let the animal shape your training protocols to maximize effectiveness.
"Make the wrong things difficult, and the right things easy."	Make an undesirable behavior inefficient for the animal to access reinforcement. Make it take more energy, take longer to complete, or delay access to reinforcement. Make the consequences of the desired behavior preferable.
"The horse tells you where he is. Work with him on his level."	It is your job as a trainer to set your animal up for success.

"The horse was trying to figure them out, but when the rider wanted more and better without even rewarding the horse for what he'd tried to do, the horse said, "This is the wrong thing to do because I get punished for this." So he quits. He bucks them off, or blows up, or freezes up, or rears.	If the (release of pressure) reinforcement is not forthcoming, the animal will get frustrated and try an alternative way to get relief.
"Your idea should become his idea, and when it does, there will be no drag."	If the horse is operating from signaled avoidance, it will be in synchrony with you.
"The horse will give you the answers and he will question you to see if you are sure or not."	Even though you have tailored your training plan to fit the temperament of the animal, the animal may still try avoidance and escape behaviors.
"The slower you do it, the quicker you'll find it – it can happen so soon you don't feel it."	A systematic approach will result in the most efficient training program.
"Try to keep his mind soft and mellow."	Optimizing the situation to avoid problematic emotional arousal is a goal of good training.
"We need to recognize the smallest try, realize the slightest change. Many of us don't know a horse is trying to do something for us until he's already done it."	Negative reinforcement is best done by shaping very, very, small approximations.

"When you don't have a soft mental attitude you don't ask anything of your horse except to relax and feel back to you, to respond with confidence."	Conditioned relaxation and systematic desensitization should be used whenever stimuli create too much arousal.
"You do not get him in the wrong attitude. You do not want him to feel you're boring him, and that what you're asking is monotonous."	A variety of reinforcers and activities will help keep your animal motivated.
"You don't pull on the horses; he pulls on you – there's a big difference."	Making the consequence solidly contingent on the behavior gives the animal control of the access to reinforcement.
"You fix it up and let him find it."	Do your antecedent arrangements to make the choices to the animal very simple.
"You've never discouraged him, you've never belittled him, you've really bragged on him and his good qualities. When he did something wrong you didn't make a big thing of it. You went along with him there, too, and showed him that wasn't too good of a thing to do – yet you didn't criticize him or hammer on him."	It is strongly recommended not to create negative emotional arousal for best results.

Chapter 20

5. Punishment: decreases behavior

5.1 **Punishment** is not just presenting aversive stimulation to an animal. Rather it is when the aversive stimulus is presented as a consequence of a behavior and that consequence reduces the chance of the behavior being performed. By this definition inflicting pain on an animal is not punishment unless it decreases a behavior. Behaviors are punished, not animals. It takes a while to change the habit to the correct use of the word. You must slap yourself every time you use the word incorrectly to help yourself remember.

5.2 The efficacy of punishment is always open to question. Even Skinner said punishment was not very effective at controlling behavior. As animals ourselves, our innate aggressive responses to threats to our well-being are instinctive efforts to punish the threat. We are pre-wired to try to punish transgressions against us. But because of our inconsistent application, we are not very effective at it.

5.2.1 The first problem with punishment is that there are competing contingencies. The undesirable behavior exists because it has a history of reinforcement. The factors reinforcing the behavior may be operating by positive or negative reinforcement.

5.2.1.1 A careful analysis of the reinforcement maintaining the behavior is necessary. If the contingencies maintaining the behavior are not addressed, the behavior will return quickly. You might get your hand slapped for grabbing cookies out of the cookie jar, but soon enough you'll be back to sneak another one.

5.2.1.2 To decrease the behavior for more than the present moment, the animal must be able to access the reinforcement it needs in other ways. Someone who wanted you to stop getting the cookies from the cookie jar, could just give you a plate full of cookies and you'd probably leave the ones in the cookie jar alone.

5.2.1.3 A situation involving a behavior that is reinforced by negative reinforcement is problematic because using positive punishment to stop it creates a condition where no matter what the animal does, it will meet with aversive stimuli. This kind of situation is likely to result in Learned Helplessness as the animal has no choice to avoid aversive consequences. Back at the cookie jar, your ugly cousin just told you that if you don't get him a cookie, he's "gonna thump you". Which is worse a hand-slap or a sound thumping?

Fear biting is another good example of this scenario. Applying an aversive stimulus to the animal for fear biting is not going to help fix the problem. Trying to punish fear biting is going to be less effective than simply working on the fear issue directly with respondent conditioning. Take away the fear and the biting will stop.

5.2.1.4 Using punishment to stop an act behavior in process may be very reinforcing for the trainer and may condition the trainer to try to use punishment more often. When it doesn't work, the trainer is naturally going to want to increase the intensity of the stimulus, but the result is damage to the training relationship. When frustration sets in, will the aversity extinguish the trainers punishing behavior or will the trainer get shaped into escalation? The animal trainer can get trapped by that tiny bit of positive reinforcement. You can expect Mom to come up with something more aversive if you continue to filch the cookies after she's yelled at you.

5.2.1.5 Neutral stimuli can be turned into conditioned punishers by consistent paring with aversive stimuli. Stimuli associated with an aversive event becomes a conditioned stimulus for a fear reaction. If the trainer becomes an aversive stimulus, the damage to the training relationship is enormous. It may take months to repair. The animal trainer starts wishing they had called in sick that day when things fell to pieces.

5.2.2 Factors that affect the efficacy of punishment: contingency, contiguity, availability of alternative sources of reinforcement, relativity of punishers, and intensity.

5.2.2.1 A good example of effective use of punishment is an electric fence which will effectively teach the animal to not touch the fence.

5.2.2.2 If every time the animal touches the electric fence, the animal receives a small shock, the animal is less likely to want to risk touching it. If sometimes the fence is turned off and the animal can reach some nice succulent grass on the other side, then the inconsistent contingency will make the fence less effective. The shock will have to be stronger.

5.2.2.3 Animals can only respond to immediate reinforcement and immediate punishment. Punishment during the behavior is more effective than punishment after the behavior. The shorter the delay, the more effective the punishment. The electric fence delivers its stimulus with perfect precision.

5.2.2.4 The aversive needs to be truly aversive. Some animals and humans seek negative attention and will work for it. The reinforcement maintaining the behavior may relate to an emotional habit or an urge to maintain a particular hormone level, almost like an addiction (ie. adrenaline junkie).Yelling at the dog from a distance may make the dog feel like you are barking with it, not against it. Aversives are relative. It could be possible that electric fences are appetitive stimuli to an electric eel. I don't know.

5.2.2.5 The intensity of the aversive stimulus is important. More intense punishers suppress the behavior more effectively. Less intensive punishers can be counterproductive because of the Weak to Strong effect; this principle says that applying weak punishers makes later strong punishers LESS effective (a problem for "escalation"). This may be because the animal has coped with it in a weak form and the animal now knows it can probably cope with the problem anytime, or it may be simple habituation. Too little intensity doesn't work and too much intensity doesn't work. The electric fence has to be stronger than a static electrical spark and weaker than a lightning bolt.

5.2.2.5.1 If you look at the electric dog training collar literature, you get a feeling for how varying the intensity of the stimulus might affect the situation. (Hint: there is a reason even the collar manufacturers say that you don't want to use more stimulus than necessary).

5.2.2.6 If you use punishment, it should be applied as if you were an electric fence. Notice that the benefits of uniformity of application are unlike the effect of variable reinforcement for positive reinforcement.

5.2.2.6.1 The problem with electric dog collars is that they are used with neither consistent contingency nor close contiguity and they don't allow the animal access to the reinforcement it is trying to access with the undesirable behavior. They are prone to malfunction. They cause negative emotional arousal and lead to avoidance of the trainer. Plus, there are better ways of getting rid of unwanted behaviors. We borrowed one, experimented with it, and then we solved the problem with Differential Reinforcement of Incompatible Behavior which is more forgiving of our personal inconsistencies.

5.2.3 Punishment requires careful application to be effective. Here are the guidelines: 1) use medium intensity to start (totally annoying but not frightening), 2) do not increase intensity, 3) deliver during the behavior if at all possible, and 4) deliver consistently for every incidence of the behavior.

5.2.4 Making Punishment Most Effective

· **Abrupt introduction and immediacy of punishment.** Consequences should be delivered immediately in a startling way to be more effective.

· **Intensity of punishment.** High intensity positive punishment may permanently suppress behavior. If the behavior starts to return, some kind of reinforcement for that behavior is supporting it. Look for a different solution.

· **Schedule of punishment.** Punishers delivered continuously are more effective compared to those delivered intermittently. Force yourself to be very consistent about this.

· **Delay of punishment.** The longer the delay between

response and punisher, the less effective the punishment will be. After 10 seconds punishment cannot be effective.

- **Motivation and punishment**. When motivation to perform the bad behavior is reduced or when the behavior is not being reinforced in other ways, punishment will be more effective. Behavior may be completely suppressed when the motivation to offer the undesirable behavior is low. When conditions change the behavior may be more tempting.

5.3 The Two Types of Punishment: 1) **Positive punishment** decreases a behavior by application of an aversive consequence.

5.3.1 The advantage of using positive punishment is that it works fast if applied consistently during the unwanted behavior. It usually interrupts the behavior immediately.

5.3.2 The disadvantage of positive punishment includes emotional arousal, avoidance behaviors, aggression, disruption of other types of operant learning, and an increased likelihood of animal abuse by the trainer.

5.3.3 Delivery of the aversive stimulus by a social agent has relationship consequences. Consider the aversive stimulus of a frown. How does it make you feel about the person that constantly tries to control you with a dirty look? It is better to arrange the consequences so the trainer doesn't deliver the aversive stimulus, the environment does.

5.3.4 In general, positive punishment is more likely to elicit aggression because it stimulates "fight or flight" responses, and the individual animal may be predisposed to stand and fight given its history, reproductive status, etc. If you do start a fight with an animal, you really don't want to lose it and it can be very hard to patch the relationship.

5.4 The Two Types of Punishment: 2) **Negative punishment** is a much better choice and is convenient for trainers using appetitive stimuli. It requires that the animal be engaged in earning positive reinforcement.

5.4.1 LRS, Time-out, and No-Reward Markers

5.4.1.1 **Least Reinforcing Scenario** (LRS) is a very mild time out of 3 to 5 seconds, where the trainer gets very quiet without interacting with the animal, then asks the animal to do something that it has a high probability of doing, so that it can be reinforced for engaging with the trainer.

5.4.1.2 A longer **Time-out** is effective for addressing unwanted behaviors which have a stronger history of reinforcement. Every time the unwanted behavior occurs, training and all opportunity to earn reinforcement stops for 5 or more seconds after the last bit of previous reinforcements have been swallowed. The time is kept short but is relative to the speed of consumption. The animal gets somewhat anxious that the session has terminated. There may be some display of extinction related behaviors such as a frantic response or aggression. When the animal has calmed down and shown a calm response, the training session begins again at a point where the animal will be immediately successful. This level of time out may require the trainer to be behind protection of the cage or pen fence.

5.4.1.3 For totally unacceptable behaviors, such as aggression, the session is simply terminated. Note that this does not apply if you are using aversive stimulus. It depends on the animal being engaged with earning something it wants. When you terminate the session, it is time to sit down and figure out a plan to deal with the problem which usually boils down to emotional arousal or frustration. It's time to get a cup of tea and let your adrenaline level get back to normal.

5.4.1.4 Sometimes we want a stimulus to signal that a behavior will not be reinforced at this time. This type of stimulus is called a "**No Reward Marker**". The words "unh-oh", "quit", "not that", "oops!", and "wrong" are frequent choices for "no-reward" markers. Application of the NRM is by definition a positive punishment even though it signals a negative punishment. These are positive punishers in that they are presented as consequences and they decrease behaviors. Many trainers choose not to use it because of its positive punishing aspect. There is a childhood game that explicitly uses this type of signal by saying the participant is getting warmer or colder as they try to determine the location of a secret object. Does the child resent the "colder" feedback?

5.4.2 The effective use of negative punishment requires extreme consistency. It helps to have it already in your mind as the backup plan when you enter the training session. It takes will power to just stop the game because training is reinforcing for the trainer as well.

5.5 There are several ways to decrease behavior beyond punishment.

5.5.1 Providing easier ways for the animal to access the reinforcement it was receiving for the behavior is very effective. If the reinforcement was getting away from the trainer, escape should be allowed if not facilitated, and then the trainer should work at making escape less appealing than playing the training game. Decreasing the motivation for the animal to perform the behavior is the first step to take because it will facilitate extinction.

5.5.2 Reinforcement of a desirable behavior can help drive the extinction of an unwanted behavior. In this combination, a replacement behavior is rewarded, while the one slated for extinction is ignored. This is called **Differential Reinforcement**.

Differential reinforcement can focus on reinforcement of any **other**, a specifically **incompatible**, or an **alternative** behavior that accesses the same reinforcer. The desirable behaviors are reinforced while the undesirable behavior is ignored. This works better than punishment. If your mom had put you to work making cookies when you wanted them, you could have been filling the cookie jar instead of emptying it.

Chapter 21

6. Scientific Attitude

6.1 Using feedback is playing the warmer/colder game. By becoming sensitive to the consequences of our behavior, we can increase effectiveness of our training. Small improvements in our animals (getting warmer) can help us to know where we are being effective. Declines or stalemated training (no change or getting colder) can let us know where we need to improve. We can use it to reinforce good practices or punish our own bad habits. However, if you don't quantify your results and train yourself to become sensitive to the feedback, you can get a lot of experience in how to get marginal results and old habits will prevent you from ever being a really good trainer.

6.1.1 If you have a tool to measure it, you can change your heart rate, your brain waves or just about anything about yourself you can't currently control. If you can measure and quantify, you have the power of science and technology at your fingertips! Your measurements need to be easy to make, but still sensitive to small changes.

6.1.2 What kind of dimensions of behavior can you measure?

6.1.2.1 Recording the number of times the behavior occurs in a given period of time results in a **frequency**. If you count the number of responses in 3 minutes and then divide by 3 minutes, you get the number of responses per minute.

6.1.2.2 Recording a) the number of times the behavior occurs, and b) the number of times the behavior was requested to occur results in a rate of response to the cue. If you cued 10 times and got the correct behavior 8 times, you have an 80% response to the cue. I call this a **rate of success**.

6.1.2.3 **Latency** (time between request and behavior) involves recording how long from the stimulus onset until behavior occurs. You need a stopwatch to do this with any accuracy, but you can certainly modify the antecedents to drive latency down to its lower limits. Graphing an average latency over several trials will be more useful than a single latency measurement.

6.1.2.4 **Duration** of behavior can also be quantified with a stopwatch; you simply record how long the behavior lasts, or its **absolute duration**. You can also use a timer and measure the frequency of the behavior lasting a given interval, or the **success rate at the given interval**. There is a difference between the results of these two approaches in that the stopwatch method will allow you to say that the average length of time that the animal will persist in the behavior is 7.5 seconds, while the timer method will allow you to say that the animal persists in the behavior for 10 seconds in 3 out of 10 tries. It is hard to reinforce correctly and measure absolute duration but easy to reinforce success at a set interval.

6.1.2.5 **Outcome** is usually a yes/no record. Did the animal fetch the ball? Did the animal offer the behavior before I cued for it? Sometimes you need more options than 2.

6.1.2.6 **Engagement** is amplitude or energy of behavior: intensity or force of a response. A quantitative measure of amplitude might be something like jumping height, but more often it is a subjective rating as if you were an Olympic judge. I gauge a lot of responses by height and use the grid provided by the fencing to make my estimates.

6.1.2.7 A **Discrimination** score can be calculated from a) the number of times a cue was offered and responded to, divided by b) the total number of cued and uncued responses. If you have a frequency of response to the cue of 100% of the time for 10 requests, but you have 50 total incidences of the behavior (40 uncued), your discrimination score is 10/50 or 20%. The animal isn't really responding to the cue at all.

6.1.2.8 **Motivation** can be recorded with a subjective score. If recorded every day, it helps to identify when an animal isn't feeling well, to assess your value as a partner to this animal, and to calibrate the portions of feed your animal is receiving.

6.1.2.9 **Suppression** is a very good thing to record for animals which are becoming tame. Measure how far away you are when the animal leaves its food because you are approaching. It is easiest if you have measurements already along your pathway and you check at each interval (foot, yard, etc.) to see if you have entered the suppression zone. You can also measure how long it takes to come back to the food. Dressing differently, offering different foods, changing deodorants, etc. may change the suppression zone distance, so you can experiment with this.

6.1.3 The **"base rate"** is the first set of measurements to take. It is the rate of response prior to training. That might be zero times a day for a behavior that you want to increase, or 10 times a minute for a behavior you want to decrease. The measurements you take later in the process can be compared to the base rate. You may have a starting base rate at the beginning of a training session and compare with the end of session. It doesn't matter that the animal already has some training. Your criterion is only that the measurement provides you a meaningful starting point to compare progress on the timescale of interest. You may be only interested in looking at the effect of arranging the objects in the training environment. Your base rate is the measurement before, so you can compare the measurement after.

6.2 Quantify and Graph

6.2.1 Recording progress can be an extremely reinforcing activity for a trainer. Keeping a simple narrative journal does not have the same immediate impact that seeing a good trend on a graph.

6.3 Treatment: what affects what?

6.3.1 A functional relationship exists between changes in the antecedent environment and the target behavior when the variable can be shown to influence the behavior. Behaviorists call the changes in the antecedent environment "**treatment**" or "**intervention**". The treatment could be any part of the antecedent conditions such different reinforcer, a new trainer, or the consequences of the last contingency. This is demonstrated when the behavior changes as a result of exposure to the treatment conditions. When the data are put on a graph, the baseline results can be compared to the treatment condition results. Typically, there would be a vertical line on the graph dividing the baseline from the treatment data. This line is called a "phase line" and each side of the phase line is labeled with the conditions it represents. Identify the parts of the graph shown below for some practice with this important topic.

94　　　　　　　　*How 2 Train A* _____

6.4 Assessing Animal Preferences. It is fun to study which alternative is more attractive to an animal by asking which is more reinforcing. Animals will tend to return to the same location so rearranging the choices is going to give a more complete picture of their preferences. If the animal starts alternating from one choice to the other you can have a small time-out every time the animal changes to control that behavior.

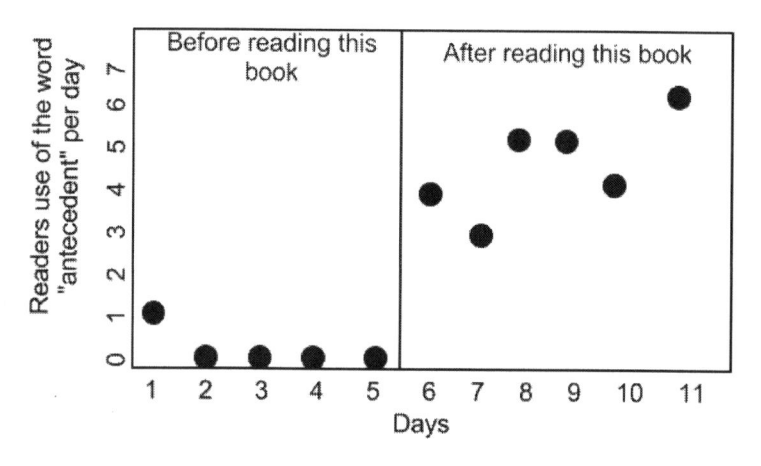

Find the 6 Essential Elements of the Graph
- X-axis (hint: days) and Y-axis
- Axis labels
- Axis numbers
- Data points (there should be 11 of them)
- Phase line
- Phase labels

If you present the results of a behavior modification project, having all six of these on your graph will add to your credibility.

Chapter 22

IMO: the Training Session

I could tell you how you can apply this information to train your animals, but I won't. Instead, here is a glimpse into my training world and my history of reinforcement. If you want to train like me, that's your choice. But whatever you do, you *will* train like you.

Chapter 22.1

Antecedents to the Session

Planning and Decisions

Long and Short Term goals for the animal

I start by making a list of *all* the things that I want the animal to end up knowing. Few people bother to do this but it's probably the biggest difference between an an amateur and a professional. My training plans are critical to me. It prevents me from training behaviors that are ultimately going to be a roadblock to something I want to train later. I have analyzed each of my cues as well, so I have less probability of trying to use one cue to mean two things. It helps me to make lists of these types of things. When I try to share my lists with training friends, they take one look at my list and recall why they consider me a training geek. My reinforcement for this activity comes from improvements in my processes, not from social approval.

I keep a list of 101 behaviors that I want my personal horses to know, and every once in a while, I take it out and test all the horses. This testing is an excellent introduction to horsemanship for a novice student, so I like to do it when I have groups of interns. Anything the animals have forgotten can quickly be brought back up to speed and the interns get a broader range of training experience. My lists also keep me heading towards a long term goal with each one of the animals. When I started keeping this master list, I started noticing details about what other people were training and their use of cues. It gave me a way to evaluate changes in my program. No, actually, it *gave* me a program. It is *that* important. Whatever kind of paradigm structured my style and dictated what behaviors should be trained before I got organized crumbled away. My world was reinvented. Suddenly ANYTHING was possible. At that point, training became really exciting!

Having clear criteria in my mind (and more so on a piece of paper in my pocket) as I head into a session helps me focus on getting the animal to meet the criteria and stay headed along the path. I stay equipped with some data collection tools (timer, pencil, paper, and counter). It's reinforcing for me to check off the tasks and to write the results into their training records. The graphs documenting improvements please me endlessly.

Having those criteria helps me also to remember why I should not reward for less than they can do. If my criteria are a little vague and I start rewarding for vaguely correct behaviors, the result is that the animal will only offer vaguely correct behaviors. Don't ask me how I know this (it's too painful to remember). I could never fix the problem by just getting stricter because the animal would get frustrated and quit trying. Fortunately there is a solution! I just pick out one new behavior to work on and train for crystalline crispness in the new behavior. For some reason, the crispness and precision usually seeps into other behaviors. When this new behavior is working well, then I can come back to the old mushy behaviors with more precision. I don't know why that seems to generalize, but it does. Latency problems seem to work the same way. The new behavior can be something very simple like targeting to a unfamiliar object, so the improvement process can actually take place in one session.

If my animal is progressing well, I push the criteria up a notch. I don't stick with minimum progress if the animal shows me it is ready for maximum. That happy state where the channels of communication has been opened is a wonderful place to train. The animal is trying to please! When this happens to me, that long list of behaviors suddenly looks much shorter. I keep a few extra goals in my pocket for those moments. In one session I might find myself finishing early but if I terminate the session the animal will not be satisfied. I can either capitalize on the moment, or just leave a little pile of food in their dish. The thing I do not want to do is bore the animal. The down side of pushing criteria is that too much can be frustrating for the animal. It's a delicate balance.

What style is going to work best for this animal?

First let's review some basics. In the Laws of Behavior section we talked about how behaviors can increase or decrease in frequency. As an animal trainer, most often I want to increase desirable behaviors and decrease unwanted behaviors. I see my job as knowing what behaviors to change and setting conditions that will facilitate the changes in the appropriate direction. It is essential to focus on one behavior at a time and to know if I want to increase or decrease this behavior. To increase a behavior, I use the principle of reinforcement. To decrease a behavior I use differential reinforcement, extinction or punishment. By breaking it down this way, it is very easy to plan my course of training.

Less frequently than changing frequencies of behavior, but more critically, I have to change the emotional reaction of an animal toward humans, myself in particular. I simply associate significant pleasant things to my presence, usually by teaching the animal to eat from my hand while relaxed. Sometimes the animal needs to feel some greater degree of control over its situation before it can relax, so I teach it that it can control me. This is the respondent conditioning part of my practice, and for what I do, which is tame wild horses, it is Mission Critical.

Now that we know where we want to get, we have to figure out the best way to get there.

The question of whether or not to include food or aversive

pressure is shockingly contentious among opposing groups of animal trainers. But many things are shockingly contentious between animal trainers. I try to avoid those discussions. I believe that animal trainers have strong histories of reinforcement, and they are not going to abandon the methods which they feel make them successful. In my own practice, I have been more successful with positive reinforcement, but I know how to use aversives as well and use them when needed. There are many ways to get a job done. If a trainer has production deadlines and an ability to restrain the animal, negative reinforcement is more likely to be an important tool in their box. If they have all the time they need or animal can't be restrained, aversive stimuli are going to be something they neither need nor want. These are choices we all have to make.

I am frequently asked about mixing negative (-R) and positive (+R) reinforcement. I do, but, if the mix is in the wrong proportions, things can deteriorate quickly. But certainly they can work together and amplify the motivation to perform a behavior. Think about addiction for a moment: with most addictive substances there is a -R in the withdrawal syndrome that is relieved by using, as well as a +R in the "high", until the user habituates to the drug and then is only driven by avoidance of withdrawal. Balancing a mix of positive and negative is delicate work and there are so many ways that things could go wrong. *Don't violate the relationship* is the guiding principle.

If my plan calls for reducing the frequency of a particular behavior, I don't seriously consider punishment except as a last resort. The first choice should be to try to diminish the reinforcement for undesirable behavior and increase the reinforcement for alternate behaviors.

Compulsion training does not work well with many types of animals. Consider the case with cats. What kind of threat would make a house cat perform a trick? Mature animals of any species are less likely to respond well to aversive stimulus. If an animal is endowed with tooth, beak, claw, or hoof, it may be more likely to respond with aggressive counter-control. Failures arising from aversive training practices are rampant. It is far too easy to just dispose of the animal, so the reality never has to set in. The bad animal trainer simply disposes of his mistakes and blames it on the "bad" animal.

The convenience of this disposal is somewhat institutionalized in the horse world. The histories of ownership for individual horses are kept rather veiled considering the lifespan of a horse. Owners don't usually expect a training history to come with the horse. A description that reads "90 days of professional training" is supposed to convey the whole story. I believe that this veiling of information intentionally protects poor quality trainers, and it is heartening to seeing that the really good trainers are marking their animals with freeze brands to say that they are proud of and stand behind their work.

There is a lot of talk about leadership and dominance in both the dog and horse training world. I think the ideas cause a lot of bad human behaviors. Dominance, in this context, is really just that status of being a potential aversive stimulus. And "leadership" seems to mean knowing what the next thing you want to do is and not reinforcing poor performance. A bad leader lets the animal get bored or doesn't make it clear where the next opportunity for reinforcement is. In my opinion, dominance and leadership are like emotional-driven behaviors in that they will suddenly just seem meaningless if we are doing good training . Once I escaped the trap of this kind of thinking, it seemed that my training repertoire grew and my results got a lot better; especially dealing with people.

Ultimately, I choose my methods to fit my style and the animals' needs. Then if I'm not getting the results I want, I change things. I try to give the needs of the animal a lot of thought and the results maintain my own training-related behavior. I never give up on an animal because I know the Laws of Behavior are totally reliable.

What does this animal need to go forward?

If I can inspire trust and control, everything else pretty much falls into place, so I don't skip over the rough spots early on and hope for things to improve. Pretending nothing is wrong won't work in most cases. I take all the time it takes to get those two elements firmly in place. Trust and control.

I find that training for alternating conditioned relaxation and focused attention is an excellent starting place. I can reinforce the postures of relaxation, and then raise the criteria by reinforcing quiet breathing, slow blinking, etc., to reach a deeper relaxation. When I can ask the animal to relax on cue, I have the ability to prevent many wrecks before they happen. Walking around with the animal and practicing relaxation in various locations is a good first way to start to introduce these animals to the bigger world. Focused attention is taught by reinforcing the animal for looking at me and then raising the criteria for the longer-duration behavior of watching me. These two things are very simple to instill in the animals once you can hand-feed them.

Although I use positive reinforcement, negative reinforcement horse trainers sometimes condition a relaxation response by tapping the animal rather forcefully and quickly until it shows the desired behavior. Yes, oddly enough they get the animal to relax by tapping it!

There are five predictable stages horses in training go through. I have winnowed down his list and generalized it to all animals, defining five fundamental stages in almost every training process for any species as discussed in Chapter 16. (1) Basic Attempt: 2) Low Latency; 3) With Duration; 4) Relaxed Engagement, and 5) With Distraction).

These five stages are just small improvements from one to the next. I see a lot of novice trainers make the mistake of expecting a finished or higher level response in the beginning, when they would profit from just encouraging the basic attempt. People don't like to start small, but it is absolutely necessary. Reward those nascent beginnings! After learning a few behaviors, the animal will soon come to realize that the criteria are going to constantly shift and there will be no misunderstanding or resentment about always changing the rules. The only time my animals seem to mind, is if I have drilled them too long at some approximation.

Hand-Feeding Issues

Many people are afraid of hand-feeding animals. People allow their animals to walk on them, push them around, or grab food from them, and then think the problem created is simply the result of delivering food by hand. From their perspective, they simply fed the animal and the animal got aggressive, so they quit hand-feeding. These people are probably truly safest if they *never do* hand-feed their animals because the people don't have the knowledge or skill to deal with it. The preferred alternative would be that the people could learn to have boundaries with their animals that require the animal to ask politely and not demand. I suspect that training with food requires the trainer to be more rational than emotional.

If you are going to use positive reinforcement you are going to need to be able to deliver the food and it will be much easier if you can do hand-feeding. I discuss getting them calm enough to hand-feed later under "Dealing with a Fearful Animal", but this is a good place to talk about the physical aspects of food delivery.

If I am training animals that are likely to bite, I would want to deliver the food in a dish or on a stick instead of with my hand. If I was feeding a carnivorous non-domestic animal, I would probably never offer food from my hand. Predatory animals are good at catching tossed bits. Some individual herbivorous animals are more likely to use their teeth than their lips, usually because of mouth physical problems, I feed these animals from a solid dish and the surface forces them to learn to use their lips to pick up the food.

Some animals will be totally creeped-out to touch a human hand. It is so naked, has claws and stinks! They will get so focused on the human appendage that they forget about the food. My best bet is to be totally passive (but ready to pull back in case they want to taste human flesh). I never reach for the animal. I don't wave the food in their faces. My hand should just be an inert food container. Some of the mustangs rustle through the hay I am offering, until they have exposed the hand holding it. They give me a scathing look as if to say, "Get that nasty thing out of my food!!!"

If the animal is at all nervous about me, when it has taken the food, I pull my hand smoothly away and retreat slightly away from the animal (to where it can be comfortable about my presence). I keep adrenaline out of the training session and the opiods in as much as possible.

Avoid setting up a roadblock

Before I train duration or change to an intermittent schedule of reinforcement I try to analyze what later behaviors it might affect. Training these two elements can affect the animal's likelihood of trialing a new behavior or a variation of a behavior. Once they learn to wait, things can get really slow. To make it clear to my animals, I use a countdown signal to train duration, as long as I am counting down they are to wait. It readily generalizes to other behaviors.

What could go wrong? Planning alternatives.

Dealing with Aggression

I have warned you previously that, in general, redirection is not a good idea, but sometimes it is a simple emergency to do so. Redirecting an animal from an undesirable behavior to an acceptable behavior doesn't actually lessen the probability of the undesirable behavior for more than a minute or two, but it might prevent a tragedy. Good targeting behaviors are invaluable when redirecting. Any animal that poses a serious threat to the trainer by virtue of size, sharpness of claw and tooth, etc. should be a stimulus for you to institute an emergency redirection plan. This is sometimes called the DRI, or differential reinforcement of incompatible behavior. A zebra who is touching his nose to my finger target cannot be kicking me at that same time. I always plan to get the dangerous part of the animal in a safe orientation or busy so it doesn't have time to ruin my day.

Having a DRI to compete with the animal's motivation to be aggressive is only as effective as the DRI's history of reinforcement. I plan my DRIs carefully and get stimulus control as perfect as possible for that one time when someone really needs it. For the wild horses, it is never too early for them to learn to stop in their tracks at the cue "whoa". The fact that this becomes one of their deepest and most reinforced behaviors is going to save someone's life sooner or later. I don't ride them, so it's not my neck, but I know training this from the start will make it more reliable when needed. If you plan a DRI, you should not wait until the animal is bolting away or attacking to use it. Practice your DRIs every day for one or two repetitions. Reward generously!

Aggressive behaviors are neurochemically self-rewarding. We can't ignore them, because they will escalate on their own. Any sign of aggression from an animal should be taken quite seriously, even if it is directed at another animal. Aggressive behaviors are often presented when the animal is frustrated and needs to vent. We can't ignore it. Our only option is to insure our personal physical safety immediately. I train through a barrier for much of the beginning of the taming process. If I am training a behavior that is challenging the animal too much and it shows any sign of wanting to find a vent for his frustration, I change what I am doing to get a high rate of reinforcement doing something the animal can be successful with. Sometimes this keeps the animal's focus on the training session and the tension melts away. If I feel that the aggression truly has nothing to do with me, but is cross-fence rivalry, I try to discourage it by short time-outs when the animal returns to the training session. For the first 10 seconds I might be busy writing notes or taking photos. They have to wait for me to "notice" they want to train.

After responding to any serious threat display by removing myself, I consider how to give the animal more control of what is happening so its level of frustration goes down. Can I back up one level of approximation criteria to make the animal successful? Can I provide the animal with more information by providing a prompt or lure? My task is to keep safe and give the animal a way to be successful.

One of the problems is that the trainer is a limited resource. If the animals really love their training time (or if they are a bit hungry), they will be quite jealous of whoever is getting the trainer's attention. I try to set up the environment so that there is no real damage done. Animals playing with each other in mock battles is a sign of good animal welfare, but animals trying to seriously hurt each other is a sign that something is wrong. It is also good to double check that they are getting enough food in their regular rations, and that it's not critical nutrition they are having to fight for.

My own way of dealing with chronic aggression toward me is to consider it as arising out of conflict within the animal. The animal is put in its own quarters where it can see and sniff other animals, and see me train other animals. I like the "problem child" to see the other animals working for and munching on reinforcers. The angry animal goes onto Food Schedule 2 (full but lower quality rations) to make the value of the reinforcer higher. Then I work through the protected contact of the cage or pen so the animal is not really a threat. I use every opportunity to stop by and train the animal for a minute. If the animal shows any aggression, I turn away, give the treat to another animal, and walk away. I let the conflicted animal tell me it doesn't want to play. Aggression means "leave me", so I do it. They get to watch me training the animals nearby. These "angry" animals normally go through a sad state of affairs where they want to get the reinforcers, but their pride doesn't let them play with me. They get even madder, making a big display of it. Then in a day or two they slip into playing for just a moment or two before they get mad. This procedure relies on the same principle of addictive behavior. Playing games with the trainer results in tasty snacks! "Yes, you have to be mad, but a quick game with the trainer wouldn't hurt."... "Okay, but just one!" Well, it's addictive and it is hard to play just one, so pretty soon, being mad is in the way of feeding the addiction. The animal learns to inhibit it's aggression in order to play the game. Ultimately the conflict that was driving the aggression dissipates, but for a while we have aggression merely under the rug where it can be brought out at any moment. So I don't think it is gone until I know for certain it is gone. I keep the training sessions short and addictive and I start working on the DRI.

Dealing with Animals that aren't doing what you want.

Sometimes the problem is that the animal won't try and seems to be just waiting for me to give them the treat. I normally see this in animals who have come from owners who just fed them treats without requiring behaviors. Donkeys are the worst! If the animal learns that it can get the trainer to lower the criteria if it waits, the trainer will probably want to feed the animal in the next pen and give the trainee a time-out. I might try to inspire a little competition between animals for my attention. Donkeys are patient beasts and getting them past this problem can take weeks.

You must ask yourself, "Does the animal want my attention? Is it reinforcing for me to look away or leave?" If you are training with negative reinforcement, giving the animal a time-out for bad behavior doesn't make sense. If you are training with positive reinforcement, the animal will not like losing the opportunity to earn reinforcement.

Many trainers purport to use a neutral response and a 5 second wait to extinguish incorrect responses, but calling them neutral and extinguishing isn't exactly correct. If it was truly neutral, then you would just ignore the behavior and go on. The animal will experience it as a punishing time-out. "If you do that, I will not play with you," is the message. I think it is more credible to recognize it as a very mild negative punishment and add a no-reward-marker to it -- "Not that!" You end up with a mild secondary punisher that by being paired consistently with a time-out can be used to tell an animal what not to do in a very polite way. It comes to mean "No reinforcement is available for that activity, try something else."

Longer time-outs, where the animal entertains itself by finding something else to do, are not very effective for changing the animal's behavior. They are, however, very effective for handling emotional arousal in the trainer. Leaving the animal when it is behaving incorrectly is a good idea with positive reinforcement but is a very bad idea when training with negative reinforcement. I repeat this point because it is critical.

It is a worthwhile goal to prevent the animal from ever practicing flight responses because practice makes permanent.

Environment Management

Among the function-altering stimuli are two classes of conditions that can be manipulated to change behavior. The setting events (or situational influences) can be adjusted to make the right behavior easier than the wrong behavior. Motivating factors, making the consequences more or less desirable can also be controlled. Antecedent control is a necessity.

Motivation

Dopamine or cortisol? You can choose your favorite neurochemical motivator[1]. Mine is definitely dopamine with a shot of oxytocin on the side. Liquid trust, yes!

We keep track of what our animals eat so we can depend that they will be at least a little bit interested in what happens to be in the trainer's pouch. It is not long into the taming of a wild animal that touch and social interaction becomes reinforcing, but at first we just don't have those options.

> The Food Management Plan
> - **Level One**: No limitation of quantity or quality of food. Work for extra treats.
> - **Level Two**: Reduced quality of rations offered (acceptable but not preferred). Work for preferred rations or treats.
> - **Level Three**: Half-rations of reduced quality rations (acceptable but not preferred) in morning, full rations at night. Work for preferred rations or treats.
> - **Level Four**: 100% hand feeding morning and night.

Distractions

Sometimes I wish I had a horse-sized sound proof operant conditioning chamber for my trainees. One facility I trained at was next to the police and road maintenance department. Sudden loud noises were the norm so much that I called the City Manager and told them they were putting my life in danger. Yikes!

---

[1] Negative reinforcement and avoidance can, though the mediation of a safety signal, also generate dopamine.

Controlling distractions is very important for two reasons. First, aversive noises seem to be synchronized with critical moments in the animal's education and dishabituation is guaranteed. This kind of random noise will put you back at square one a million times. Secondly, it has been proven that animals trained without distractions learn so much faster that later, in the face of distractions, they can outperform animals that received the same training, but with distraction. The accelerated rate of progress that training without distractions produces is very reinforcing to the trainer. Once the training is getting solid, the distractions can be introduced in a gradual way.

I am careful to examine the environment for factors that might hamper success. I control what I can.

One factor that is often overlooked by neophyte trainers is how you smell. Just because your olfactory apparatus is insensitive, doesn't mean that the animal doesn't notice. Perfume, strong soaps, etc. are aversives. There was a young man who came to learn about training horses but he liked to wear essential oils. I told him the horses would prefer that he washed it off, but he didn't take my advice seriously and a few days later left feeling that horses didn't like him. I didn't either. One of my training colleagues says that there are essential oils that will calm horses down, but every time I offer to test it if she will send me a sample, she forgets to do it. I remain skeptical. We really don't know much about the olfactory worlds our animals live in, but it is wise to give it some consideration.

Cues

Everything has the potential to become a cue stimulus. The way we move, the angle of each part of our bodies, our sounds, etc. The animal doesn't realize that we just want it to notice what our hand is doing; instead it notices the angle of our arm, how our feet are lined up, our hair moving in the breeze, etc. I take the time to analyze the other potential stimuli that I am presenting to the animal when I offer them a cue. I know that I make faster initial progress if I keep everything that is not actually the cue exactly the same until I am certain that the animal notices the intended cue. I can relax the delivery after the animal has figured out what it needs to watch.

It helps me to remember to keep the cue connected to the behavior. I pick cues that are likely to elicit the behavior even without training. I might use body language, focus, or my voice. I try to send my energy in the direction I want the animal to move. I invite.

Cue discrimination is taught by putting the previously learned selected behavior on cue (or associating it with a stimulus). Then other cues for other behaviors are offered. If the selected behavior is offered in response to some other cue, the no-reward marker is given and there is a brief time-out. If the correct behavior (selected or other) is offered, then I reward and congratulate the animal, and the game goes on. This is trickier than it sounds. I try to make it very, very simple at first.

Carefully examine the cue you are planning to use. Is it likely to elicit fear in itself? You can use respondent conditioning to make it less threatening and more interesting to the animal. Pair presentation of the cue object with a reinforcer for a few times before you start on using it as a cue. This is particularly important with things such as flags, whips or guider wands. I try to build a positive association by using the cue object as a target before I use it as a cue. By making it a target, the animal stays sensitive to it as a stimulus, but not fearful of it.

Being extremely specific with motions and body angles gives animal trainers the option of relatively similar cues for a variety of different behaviors, distinguishing between the behaviors by the nuances of the signal given. We can multiply the number of cues associated with hand signals by attending to arm angles and types of motions. The animal's propensity to be sensitive to these specific details of the presentation can be a challenge when we need to have a generalized cue that can be presented with the opposite hand, from a different relative position, or even by a different person.

Prompts are by definition antecedent stimuli that increase the chance that the cue will lead to the appropriate behavior. This can include verbal, physical, visual things such as lures and bigger cues. Prompts are okay, but lures cause problems. They focus the animal on getting the food instead of thinking about what it is doing to earn the food. If I use a lure, it's because I need more respondent conditioning to get the animal past its reservations about performing the behavior. An example of this would be offering the animal food in the corner of the pen to make the corner of the pen seem like a safe place to be. I don't use lures when I don't need the respondent effect because they generally distract the animal from learning. Bribes are a whole different topic, but a bribe is given before the behavior, and that doesn't work at all!

Session Lengths and Training Time

Session management can be handled in three ways: train for a set short amount of time and have several sessions per day, train until you lose the animal's attention, or train until you reach a criterion. Negative reinforcement trainers are the most likely to train until they reach a criterion. Training in multiple short sessions whets the animal's appetite for interaction. Training until the animal looses an attention span is a big commitment with a large food-motivated animal but probably the best option for a small animal that is not an opportunistic feeder.

There is a very dangerous model out there in the horse training world where three big-name clinicians (chosen for how much of crowd they will bring with them) are given three hour-long sessions with an unhandled animal. Then they have an obstacle course they have to ride. It is all televised. Sometimes the best horse trainer wins, but there are other criteria apparently because that doesn't always happen. The viewing public gets it in their minds that based on what they see, that a trainer only needs about 3 hours to train a horse to ride. My opinion is that this kind of thing is very good for the training clinicians because it encourages people to create dangerous intractable situations that the clinicians can get paid to help fix. The clinicians just have to skillfully reinforce the horse owner for caring about their animals, being a valuable person, etc., and the person will be a good customer for life buying all the gear, books, videos, and shows the clinician produces. Without actually fixing the animal! If the animal was no longer a problem, the clinician would lose the customer.

A parallel to this would be if society said that a young person should get only 15 minutes of driving instruction. Then there was an industry set up to profit from the accidents generated. Using the left turn signal? Well, you are doing great despite that little accident. You and your car make such a great team, but you'll need to buy our other DVD to learn to use the turn signal. Go to our website. We take credit cards.

The cowboy wisdom rails against this: "the slower you go, the faster you'll get there." I would suggest that when using negative reinforcement, 3-7 correct repetitions of a new behavior are enough for a session. Then practice things that the animal is competent with. Allow a lot of time between sessions (as least as much as the session took to complete). Let the neurochemistry have time to gel. I mean that literally, it's a physical growth process.

My goal is to challenge the animal, but keep it successful. I make sure that the animal understands what is requested and is physically capable of completing the task. If anxiety is a barrier, then it is my job to work on that through emotional management. The success or failure of the training session is the success or failure of the trainer, *not of the animal*.

Chapter 22.2

Training Procedures in Action.

Dealing with a Fearful Animal: Respondent Conditioning.

CONDITIONED RELAXATION. The most effective way of desensitizing an animal to a stimulus is to pair it to a positive experience by respondent conditioning. The second most effective method is to teach the animal to assume a relaxed posture on cue, then expose the animal to the stimulus you wish it to be desensitized to in an approach / retreat method. For this, the stimulus is brought toward the animal (often from long distances) until the animal starts to show signs of vigilance. The approach stops there and the animal is coached to get into a relaxed posture. When it assumes the relaxed posture, the stimulus is immediately taken away and a treat can be fed. About 10 seconds later, the stimulus is advanced toward the animal again until the animal shows any sign of vigilance. This cycle is repeated, coming closer and closer, until the animal's principle reaction to the stimulus is to relax. Putting relaxation on cue has many benefits for desensitizing animals to stimuli.

OVERCOMING SUPPRESSION. If you can walk up to the animal while it is eating and it calmly keeps on task, you don't have to overcome much fear. But if, upon your approach, the animal goes into a state of vigilance, moves away from the food, and prepares for action, fear of you is suppressing normal behavior. You might want to measure this suppression. How close can you come before feeding is suppressed (the vigilance zone)? How far away does it move? If it's hugging the far side of the cage, that measurement might as well be infinity. How long do you have to stand perfectly still before the animal comes back? Once you quantify it, you can start driving those numbers down.

After the animal has finished its food and has developed a little appetite, you can start using respondent conditioning to associate yourself with something pleasant. You are going to become Pavlov's bell. Edge some food into the cage or pen and slip back out of the vigilance zone. Stand with your side to the animal and try to keep your lips covering your teeth. Wait quietly for the animal to come to the food and eat it. Talking, moving, etc. will just slow the process to the point where you will give up. Just wait and watch. The first step is to get the animal to take the food and come back when you resupply it in exactly the same place. When the animal is comfortable eating the food with you far away, move the food location by a few inches, with the goal of having the animal generalize about where the food will be delivered. Keep moving the food delivery point as the animal gains confidence. Soon the animal will not be hesitating to come and chow down.

When the animal is ignoring you and the food, the session is over. It is better to leave and come back for a hundred tiny sessions than it is to allow the animal to practice ignoring you. When you come back, start where the animal was half a session ago and if that is not far enough start from the beginning again. Don't be frustrated if you have to start over 20 times. The time you take with this step will be returned to you 100-fold, even if it takes weeks. If you are like me, it will help you to have a line of animals to work instead of one animal to obsess about. I just move along and they quickly learn that the approach of the human means a food opportunity is about to happen. The key is making yourself be the least aversive stimulus that you can become.

When the animal is coming right up to the food, it is time to linger nearer to the cage and wait for the animal to look at you before you put the food in. Soon you have a channel of communication established. When you get this working, the animal looking at you means he's ready for you to put the food in. The animal understands this kind of thing. Now he has some control. If he doesn't look at you, just move away and come back in a minute or two. If he won't look for three times in a row, end the session and come back later. If you need to take a break when things are working well, there will be some regression in the training level, expect it. I leave a small gift of some extra food as I am leaving and hope they miss me while I am gone.

My next step is to again raise the criteria for food delivery. I might set it at "the animal should look at me and take one step in my direction". A step away by the animal calls for a time out of 10 seconds or more with me leaving the immediate area, so I can re-approach the animal. Soon the animal will be up to the cage or pen wall, remain relaxed, and I can start handing food directly to it.

An alternative that works well for very reactive animals that may have experienced severe stress is to try to raise their nutritional status by supplying a dish with a variety of tasty bits in a quantity that will make sure they are not feeling deprived. Try to supply such a healthy assortment that any vitamins they may be short of will be replenished. For the horses I work with, I might supply 4 kinds of hay, some fortified pelleted food, and a bit of grain. Serve in a quantity that they can finish with you standing nearby. Notice which parts they eagerly eat so you can offer it to them by hand when they are ready for that step. The animals will quickly start to appreciate the banquet-delivery-organism. It won't be long before you can hand the animal its preferred flavor.

Overcoming any prior history of negative associations is important for the human hand. If your animal has been handled by other humans, it is likely to be afraid of contact. I keep a pile of old gloves to throw into a food pile the animal can rummage through. After the animal has quit worrying about the gloves, I can put one of the gloves on my hand. The gloved hand might now function as a food container. Soon though, we want to start a respondent conditioning process and make the hand mean good things. A trained animal will become very tuned into your hands if you are hand-feeding.

Some people believe that if you "provide leadership" their animal will grow confident and fear will drop away. Is this leadership more than just an acquired status as a potentially threatening stimulus? Aren't we really just talking about fostering avoidance behaviors? The horse-training advice to make them run until their lungs tell their brain to find some better thing to do is totally inhumane for fearful animals. They will run themselves to death. Their lungs don't give out. They die of exhaustion-induced myopathy where the muscles die in the accumulated waste products of exertion.

There is a scenario in which I use negative reinforcement to overcome fear. When an animal cannot even begin to tolerate humans and I have no possible way to introduce positive reinforcement, I will teach the animal that it has total control of me using the least possible aversive stimulus I can devise. Giving the animal control and predictablilty is my best bet.

Operant Conditioning

This book is not the place to find out how to train Fido to sit. Your Fido might be a crocodile for all I know. There are thousands of very useful training videos available as DVD's or free on YouTube for all kinds of species. Hopefully, through this book, you have learned enough to recognize what is really training, what is fake, and how to understand what you see. The snake-oil salespeople will want you to believe that they, and they alone, possess the real mojo, but they have been seriously reinforced for saying that. There are endless ways to learn about animal training.

Shaping

I am careful to shape one quality or dimension at a time. If the changes between the approximations are big, it is called "lumping" and is a common barrier to shaping success. I keep my animal successful with tiny graduations no matter whether I am training with positive or negative reinforcement.

In order to shape behavior, the trainer needs to carefully observe for variation in the behavior and recognize variation in the direction of desired change. Making a list of expected approximations is helpful. If the animal is showing fluency at one approximation, it is important to move on to the next, otherwise the animal will get "stuck" in a pattern. If the animal is not able to make the transition to the desired approximation, the best option is to back down to the last fluent one and reward any variation toward the higher criterion. If the animal is failing, the trainer is almost certainly asking for too much change.

Whether you are shaping with +R or –R, do not linger on an intermediate approximation. For a high-production trainer, three really good responses is usually enough fluency to move to the next step. They know that the animal will get more frustrated with stair-step progress than tiny unending transitions. This teaches the animal to keep looking for the next criteria. What the animal learns in the process will help them to learn for the rest of their lives. I monitor the rate at which they will repeat the behavior and the percentage of the cued requests that get a correct response. If the wild horses can do something seven times a minute without making a mistake, it is time to move on. If I am training an animal that has no fear issues, then the three correct responses in a row is enough.

Chaining

Behavior chains can be difficult to manage. Errors in a single link of the chain are hard to correct, so it starts being hard to not reward for sloppy delivery while still keeping the whole chain going. As good trainers add links, they make sure each behavior is rock solid before adding another link.

If all of the behaviors in a chain are taught and cued independently, when the animal is fluent, they can be chained from either direction.

Many trainers prefer to chain from the last behavior forward in order to take advantage of the Premack Principle. The first taught behavior becomes a reinforcer for the next behavior. When you start using behaviors as reinforcements, keep in mind that the behavior can only be as reinforcing as its history of reinforcement.

Teaching a horse to bow is one of those chained behaviors that has to be taught in a forward direction because the horse has to get its feet in position before it can lower its body. The first behavior I teach the horse is to put its right nostril next to its right hoof. Then I teach the horse to hold up its left hoof under its belly and extend the hoof backwards. If I get the right nostril on the right hoof and the left hoof being thrust towards the back legs, the horse usually just bows out of convenience to itself. Then I give a multiple bite jackpot and make a big deal out of it.

How 2 Train A _____

day, I got a few minutes to improvise a chained behavior a beautiful blue and gold macaw. I made the clink of a washer dropping into a tin cup into a secondary reinforcer. Then I taught the bird to make its own bridge sound by letting it drop the washers into the cup. Then I had the bird learn a simple behavior to earn a washer, which it could deposit in the clinking tin cup and get a food bit. This beautiful animal was very happy to be working for some coin. I am pretty sure I could have taken her to Las Vegas and taught her to use a slot machine.

Rewards Training

I use four fundamental tools to teach a behavior to an animal: a signal, a target, a bridge and a reward. Some people don't use a target. I don't know why.

Target

Actually, you would have to be crazy to NOT use one! A target can quickly tell the animal where and how to do a behavior. Using a target simplifies so much, that it feels like cheating! Being somewhat of an old hippy, a finger V-sign (peace sign) makes a perfect target for me. I always have it in my hand.

Animals can quickly learn to target various body parts with a pointing target and a verbal cue. A relaxed animal can learn to do this faster than I could imagine. My white hinny learned to target 10 different parts of his body to my hand in less than 20 minutes. The mistake I make in teaching this behavior is to sometimes do too much reaching and not letting the animal do the moving. That is part of that "vaguely correct" personal issue of mine that so many of my animals have been allowed to have. I am improving though.

Targeting to desensitize an animal to touch helps in two ways: 1) the animal maintains control, and 2) the tactile experience of contact with the human becomes a secondary reinforcer. How cool is that! Targeting followed by count-down-petting (CDP) is a great confidence building game to play with a shy animal. The animal gets to initiate the interaction by moving to touch the trainer. With a very confident animal you can dispense with targeting as the initiator sequence and go to count-down-petting. What is CDP? Verbally it sounds like "5, 4, 3, 2, 1, D" (D is the bridge) with a petting stroke simultaneously with each number. I vary whether I stroke on the bridge or present the reward in order to prevent too much anticipation from starting bad behaviors.

To fade a target, I practice a bit of choreography with the target, moving it and my body the same way time after time, until the animal is fluently responding, then I just set the real target aside and use the same body movements as if I was still holding it. The chances are my animal will respond correctly to the new "invisible" target.

Stationing (or targeting to a station) gives the animal a predictable place to be. Make sure that the location is comfortable for the animal. I train the horses to station with their left jaw next to my right shoulder. The wild ones learn to do this before they have ever had a rope or halter on them. It looks impressive but is actually very simple to train.

Bridge

Sometimes I bridge prematurely, and find myself in the problematic dilemma of having bridged for a seriously incorrect behavior. Crikey!!! Then I have a big dilemma. Should I compound the problem by giving the reward to an animal that has just done something I really don't want it to ever do again! I used to believe that I should withhold the reinforcement. Now I do the "slow roll".

Recall that the speed of learning is proportional to the speed of reinforcer delivery. I lapse into slow motion, dropping all but a few crumbs in the process. The animal watches me impatiently as I savor the beauty of the slow-roll. So far (I just started doing this a few months ago) it seems to solve the problem of keeping the animal motivated to try, keeping the bridge informative, and not really reinforcing bad behavior. Just yesterday, Cutter John, a very shy mustang, wanted to use his lips instead of his nose to touch my finger target. I needed to keep him trying. The slow-roll was perfect. Lipping me was soon not as attractive as getting me higher on his face.

When I have stimulus control and I am working with an animals that poses no dangers, I can simply use negative punishment (remove opportunity for earning food) and wait for the animal to stop offering the behavior before I ask for the behavior again. With horses who can be dangerous when frustrated, I find it is useful instead to have two separate behaviors to bounce back and forth, keeping that animal engaged. The one that is cued for at the moment gets a bridge and the one that wasn't requested gets a No-Reward-Marker ("Oops!"). It seems to clarify the issue for the animal to have the bridge and the no-reward-marker providing constant feedback about the contingencies for reinforcement. This doesn't happen automatically, but if I am consistent, the animal learns to monitor my feedback in just a few minutes. Oops!

Reward

I study my animal's preferences to know what it finds reinforcing. Food, toys, games, petting, scratching, heat? Carrots, alfalfa, apples, oats? Scratches on the neck, on the withers, on the rump? Any of them might be a reinforcer for an individual animal. To qualify for the list, a reinforcer must be something an animal will work for. Wild animals are reinforced by food. They all understand it, but not all animals will eat all foods. For example, wild horses don't eat things like apples, carrots, or grain. Look at your wild animal and see what it eats in nature. Sardines turned out to be what really turned my raven on. Sardines and cheese-crumbs.

The National Association of Pot Bellied Pigs says that rewards should be 1/40th of the full days ration. When I saw that presented as a fact, I wondered how they got that number and if I could translate it into work with horses. I suspect that it came from the marine mammal world where you need to have a certain number of fish for the day. Horses can eat about 10 bites a minute for about an hour (600 bites). Some species will get tired of eating and some will get overweight. Everything must be adjusted to fit the situation.

Remember that you are generating appetitive neurochemistry? It turns out that the process works much better with small rewards delivered in rapid succession. Big treats given less frequently don't generate the dopamine we are looking for, or give the animal a burst of opiod satisfaction which will decrease motivation. Even if you want to offer a super-reward or jackpot for exceptional behavior, deliver it in a succession of rapid fire small bites.

Sloppy delivery, with food falling to the ground, provides your animal access to reinforcement for ignoring you and eating the dropped bits. Some people call this **"bootleg reinforcement."** In a perfect world, you would avoid this. I use hay, so it is not possible to have a discrete bite-sized piece in my pouch. Sometimes I carry a tiny rake if I might have to do a time-out.

To keep the animal motivated, I learned to not show frustration when the behavior is incorrect. I simply encourage the animal by giving the No-Reward-Marker in response to the error quickly and reopening the game. Kind of the same behavior as a casino card dealer – no time to regret your losses; let's go again! The animal is an easy mark. The fact that your animal is still trying is worth a lot. When it does the behavior on the first (next) try, I give larger reward. The animal needs to believe that it is going to win a door-prize.

I always try to balance the effort (whether physical or mental) it takes the animal to do the requested behavior with the magnitude of the reward (keeping in mind two small bites is worth a lot more to the animal than one large bite though the quantity is the same). If there is a problem with getting the horse to actively do something (like stick its head into the halter), I start offering them little challenges with double or nothing prizes, explicitly telling them what they could win. They seem to get into a gambler's state of mind when I announce the stakes. They might win two or three small bites in rapid succession. The variability seems to take their mind off of their fears and get them engaged.

The continuous schedule of reinforcement is used to start new behaviors. But don't get stuck with a continuous schedule because it will demotivate both your animal and you with a lack of progress. Thin out your reinforcement schedule as you go.

Having too much predictability in the reward schedule is problematic. I vary the time, the number of repetitions requested, and especially the location if the animal is moving.

My student trainers have to be reminded that they stopped and rewarded the horse in the same place three times in a row and now the horse thinks that is what happens in that spot. If they aren't conscious of it, they could get upset because the horse now stops there on its own.

I ask for behavior when the animal seems to be looking for my attention and is ready to engage. I don't try to cajole it into giving me its attention by calling it repeatedly or snapping my fingers endlessly. I don't want them to practice ignoring me. I'll leave, sometimes feeding the treats to the animal in the next pen. Then I let desire grow. Short windows of opportunity promote an immediate interest in the game.

Useful games I incorporate into my practice:

INITIATOR SIGNALS. Initiator signals are a signal from the animal saying that it is ready to play the training game. If I give the animal the ability to start or stop the game, the animal seems to make a commitment to tolerate crazy trainer requests for the moment. It is as if the animal says, "Okay, give me your best shot!" Of course, I stop immediately if the animal goes into a vigilance posture and wait for the animal to re-initiate the game. The initiator signal is a power-tool for building trust.

TOUCH-IT GAME. If I can take the time to teach the animal to play the Touch-It game, new stimuli become interesting game objects. I just make it a habit to take a few novel objects with me to the training pen everyday to offer as nose targets. Then when the animal and I are outside, any unfamiliar kind of object can be used as a nose target. Pretty soon everything is a lot more interesting and a lot less scary. We have also used a mini-frisbee as an Anti-Panic button, where we placed it in various locations including on top of scary things and then reinforced the animal for touching it with its nose.

PARTY ANIMAL. If I have a group of people at my place, I round everyone up for a stall party in the middle of the mustang's training. One person goes in and starts playing face targeting games with the horse. Then a second person slips in and the animal learns to go back and forth between them. They call the animals name and say "target face" offering the target. When two people are doing alright, the third slips in and so on.

We keep distributing ourselves around the stall and if the animal gets nervous and starts running, we all step to the middle. That is a rare event because by this time the animals have a lot of reinforcement history with humans. The horse learns that when his name is called, he should look for the human offering the target. It's a great way to get them to generalize about humans being an interesting species. This can be done with any species to promote generalized human friendliness.

Pressure/Release Training

Modulating pressure improves with experience. When initiating the pressure for negative reinforcement, it is imperative to start with light pressure to avoid a fear response. By the same tolken, the aversive stimulus should be constant or nearly so. It should be annoying to the animal, but not hurt him. The trainer should never hurt the animal. Never!!

In negative reinforcement, it is imperative to give the release as soon as the behavior happens. That is the only way the animal can learn what it is doing to relieve the pressure. This requires the trainer to be organized to release the pressure in a heartbeat. The removal of the aversive stimulus needs to be almost simultaneous with the desired behavior.

It helps to mark the correct behavior with a bridge. This bridge will become a safety signal that the horse will value. I like the word "good" because people will instinctively use it correctly.

In 2010, I spent the second half of the year living at the US Forest Service mustang hold pens working to gentle the 70 horses they caught that year. It was an exciting time as I found myself totally immersed in the greatest adventure of my life. During the early months I tried out a lot of different methods recommended for mustangs to see what worked best. Negative reinforcement has a certain allure, its masters make it look like it's easy. I noticed a very interesting phenomenon that happens when I was training with negative reinforcement. The animal usually tries resisting or evading the pressure. So, for example, when I put pressure on a rope around its neck there might be kind of a wild west scene with the horse running around trying to escape the rope. Then the cell phone rings. I answer it.

The horse stops pulling the rope and just stands next to me, listening to the conversation. I call this a Cell Phone Moment. When I would finish talking and close the phone, the horse would be just obediently waiting for me. The lesson I took away was that if an animal is acting emotionally, it's probably a good idea to totally take my focus off him and make a phone call while I am at it. (*What does it really mean that that the horse does better when I quit training it? That doesn't sound very good to me! No wonder I found other ways to train.*)

The cowboy pressure/release trainer I would most recommend to study is Brian Neubert. He made some DVDs, and I particularly recommend the one about mustang gentling. There are a lot of trainers who use too much aversive pressure for my taste. Another very consistent negative reinforcement trainer is the mule trainer, Brad Cameron. Understanding the good work happening within a different training paradigm is the basis of a complete understanding of animal training. I require my students to watch a variety of typical horse training videos and analyze the techniques demonstrated. We can learn from everyone!

Punishment

In most cases, it is best to limit the opportunity for the animal to practice the unwanted behavior; however there is an alternate plan that works for seriously entrenched and reinforced behaviors. I might put them on stimulus control, and then never cue for the behavior again. Xenophon, the ancient Greek horse trainer, recommended this procedure in the 3rd century B.C. and I learned it from him. The first time I used this principle it was to use negative reinforcement to teach a horse to rear. The horse had become very dangerous for riding and was given to me as hopeless. I trained her from the ground and since she already had the habit, it really took no training at all. Then we practiced it far more times than the mare wanted. It took all the reinforcement out of it. We only did it about twenty-five times from the saddle and then I never requested it. She didn't ever try it again for the many years that I owned her. You can also train the undesirable behavior with positive reinforcement and then put the behavior on a very stingy schedule of reinforcement and never cue for it. Horse trainers often use the negative reinforcement form of this principle to get the horse to quit running away from them by making them run faster and for longer than the horse really wanted, running in a circle in a bounded space. It's a punishment because it decreases a behavior, but the behavior is what the animal chose to do, not what it was forced to do (at least at first). Pretty soon that choice is not too attractive and all the reinforcement is gone. This method should not be used with either true fear or behaviors that are intrinsically self-rewarding.

Behaviors that are driven by emotional arousal often just disappear once the emotional environment changes. Some horse trainers advocate a 3-second response to any act of aggression, they beat the animal up for three seconds anyway they can (except don't touch the face). If the aggression was fear driven, does it seem reasonable that beating on the animal is going to improve the situation? We really need to bootstrap ourselves out of these old rote training practices and use our knowledge to address problems rationally. If the animal is seriously afraid of humans, I give it some protection by training through a panel or cage. I want to give it a reason to trust me. The fear-driven aggression will go away on its own. I really don't want to become a potentially aversive stimulus in the eyes of my animals so I agonize about things before I resort to punishment (we will visit this topic later).

If a trainer uses negative reinforcement, they will be potentially positively punishing some kind of behavior every time they apply the pressure. Sometimes the behavior being punished is a non-response to the signal for avoidance. That is not a terrible thing to punish. What is terrible is to apply the aversive stimulus when the animal is innocently minding his manners or worse yet, trying to please the trainer. When I use negative reinforcement, I am very careful to signal for avoidance first and then the application of the pressure punishes ignoring the signal. That is the way to make it fair.

Time-outs and the LRS are both very mild punishments if the animal doesn't really care, but if you have an entrepreneur animal on a roll, a time-out is hard for them to endure. Take as much responsibility as you can for the communication breakdown and keep that animal engaged. An entrepreneur animal should never be discouraged.

I would be lying to you if I said I never use physical punishment. If a horse isn't afraid of me and tries to double-barrel kick me, I have no problem with defending myself. I've never had any other kind of animal try to hurt me. The horses that are prone to kicking behavior are foals and yearlings whose mothers are rather tolerant of their misbehavior. The foals merely try it out to see what happens. I just interrupt the action in the moment and then forget it. The youngster rarely tries it twice as they found nothing reinforcing about it. If I can't just "bop and stop" then I need to make a plan to train an incompatible behavior.

Chapter 22.3

Trainer Behaviors in My Repertoire.

A person might have all the knowledge to be an animal trainer and still be a dismal failure if they don't manage their own behavior. It looks kind of easy to be out just playing with the animals but if you aren't operating at 110% total self-control, you are going to be doing things and then asking yourself "why in the world did I just do that?" It is necessary to be extremely focused to do good animal training. If I am distracted, sick, tired, or grumpy, it's better to not train animals at all. I also find that having a plan written down and in my pocket will keep me from lapsing into some non-productive training just because it is more fun. On the other hand, having a self-reinforcement plan that includes a cup of tea helps maintain my data recording behavior.

Since I train people to train animals, I have seen a lot of ways to go wrong that might not be obvious. There are personal habits that get in people's ways. People with an irregular gait will make some animals nervous especially if they drag one leg against the other or maybe step flat-footed with one foot but not the other. A wild sensitive animal might not work out for these people. Then people that try to give their animal a big toothy smile are another interesting problem. They might just be trying to be friendly, but showing your teeth is not a friendly behavior between non-primates. Habitual sniffers (snorters) can really set an animal on edge. Over-caffeination is disastrous. The same kinds of annoying speech patterns (intonation, inflection, pitch, and volume) that are unpleasant to our ears are usually annoying to the animals. These kinds of things can double or triple the amount of time it takes to train a wild animal.

What I do if one of my students has an issue with personal habits is video them, show them the problem, and then use TAG training to cultivate a better habit. In TAG training, the coach marks the correct behavior just as if they were doing positive reinforcement training... well, it *is* R+, but reinforcer delivery is not necessary. First my students can work with a full length mirror and then in a real training session. The big reinforcement for them comes from the animals not being afraid of them anymore.

Sometimes making the decision to reinforce a particular instance of behavior is excruciatingly difficult. The good thing is that it becomes a moot point in three seconds. So for a second or two, there is an intense pressure to make the RIGHT decision. WHAM! It's already over and let's just pray it was the right decision... but it's already happening again!! Some people have a hard time with the stress of non-stop crucial decision making. For them, it's good to train a very forgiving animal or better yet, a human until they feel some fluency. As in the acquisition of many skills, nature says we should turn things we want to learn into a game.

I push the students to squeeze every possible excess microsecond out of the time between behavior and consequence by having them practice on me. If they are not quick, they will have reinforced me for doing something they didn't want me to do. If they just want to practice on their own, they can go practice delivering bridges with the drippy faucet, trying to bridge as it is falling before it splashes. It's just a mechanical skill so this is easy to improve.

Allow yourself to be shaped.

The cowboys put it this way: "Let the horse show you." It's all that same idea of responding to what the animal is doing, not just doggedly doing something over and over because you are sure it should work in principle. People get really stuck when they stop looking at what the animal is telling them.

Consistency is Absolutely Critical

The operant chamber is a pretty good model of consistency. The stimulus is always identically presented; the reward is always consistently delivered as predicted. Consistency goes a very long way towards getting good results.

I try to be consistently clear in how I ask for a behavior, supplying adequate information for the animal to know how to respond. But I try to be unpredictable about which behavior I might request, when I might request it, and what I will reward it with. This balance of consistency and unpredictability will keep my animal's interest going. When I am training with positive reinforcement, I want to be like a quirky vending machine. When I am training with negative reinforcement, I want to be like a bossy and adventurous best friend.

It takes discipline to work on problems. It takes discipline to turn things into a game! People with a high level of natural self discipline can excel at animal training because they will take the time to get the behavior just the way they want it. They will build a history of reinforcement in such a seamless way that the behavior is flawless. The rest of us will have just assumed they were only playing a game with that animal.

Body Language

What drives me crazy is how my dog, Roy, can walk into a pen full of wild horses, sniff a few noses and have made friends. I am convinced that he is a master of body language. First, look at his posture. It's low profile, nose to the ground. Then because he has a docked tail, there are no waving appendages for the animals to worry about. His body movements, as he casually sniffs from dung pile to dung pile, are not in the least predatory.

Humans have a lot of challenging physical attributes we have to hide to appear to be benign. We are amazingly erect. We have appendages that move in strange ways. Instead of remaining in contact with the earth, we flail them about. A bird at least folds them when not in use. We are big predators, we behave like it (we show our teeth) and we don't even know it! We just walk right up and want to touch! We have a lot of qualities in common with a *Tyrannosaurus*. Yikes!!! No wonder the animals are suspicious about us.

Some students need a lot of stress-free practice to be comfortable with a wild animal. I send my students indoors to practice in front of mirrors. It's very helpful for them to see what it looks like as they move from posture to posture. I try to make them conscious of how snappy movements generate a totally different mood than flowing gestures. People with little animal experience tend to move their hands very fast and erratically. Suddenly they realize that they do look like different animals depending on whether they are facing right or left. The animals don't generalize much, in my experience. My right side might be friendly, but they are not sure about my left side. They can't take chances until they get a little bit more experience with me.

The best way to clean up body language is to sit a camera at the eye height of the animal you are training, and then go through all the body movement issues you can think of. Perform your cues and display your moves. Then review the video and see where you can clarify your requests, drop confusing movements, and become more consistent. A TAG coach can really speed things up.

Controlling your own emotions

As human animals we are all subject to the same kind of emotions our animals are. We get reinforced when we meet with success and frustrated when we don't. If we are frustrated long enough, we will give up with some kind of rationalization of why we didn't want to do that anyway. I find it helpful to remind myself that I am only working on one behavior with one animal. This animal might be having a hard time or I might not be performing up to my own standard. I start searching for the key to improvement for that situation, hoping to learn something profound in the process. I learn more from hard animals than from easy animals. Your own personal tolerance for coping with challenge is going to dictate your choice of animals.

The second major emotion trainers feel is fear. Getting out of the pen after the animal shows signs of aggression and taking time to assess the situation gives the adrenaline (both human and other) a chance to dissipate. We can all respond more deliberately without being wired on fear. Rational judgment may be impaired by adrenaline. A trainer in this kind of situation needs to figure out how to radically improve the situation before they go back in. They need to meditate on why they didn't see it coming so they could have stopped it before it happened.

Advocating for the Animal

A lot of people just head into a training session with some random training habits they acquired somewhere in their lives. They start interacting with the animal with no plan. This is especially true with horse trainers. They don't know what they are looking for, they are using pressure but often without understanding the concept of release, and then they don't see the horse trying because they aren't getting a perfected behavior. The horse gets frustrated and emotional, then things quickly get out of hand. I can't help but feel sorry for animals who are being abused by ignorant humans in the name of training. I do what I can to encourage other people to plan for success. I offer them positive feedback for having a plan and being able to explain their objectives. Abrasive words from me about their methods never have worked to change things. Their animal failing is probably abrasive enough. If I try to motivate them to change, it backfires on me and they get more entrenched in their position. Modeling success is my best bet. Secondly, I try to reinforce them for planning their training in detail (most people are comfortable telling you their plans). It is very important to recognize their tries and keep encouraging them to train in the best way they can. The animals will be the beneficiaries of any efforts to raise the consciousness of trainers about the efficacy of their practices. If you merely recognize and salute trainer consistency, that, in itself, will help many animals down the road.

Instinctual Appeasement?

Recent studies of Post Traumatic Stress Disorder (PTSD) in humans is spinning off information which can be applied to animal training. Dr. Chris Cantor, a psychiatrist in Australia, examined the role of appeasement in complex PTSD and it's widespread occurrence throughout the vertebrate kingdom. Appeasement is considered a defence strategy between social animals of the same species (defence against non-predators). If a subordinate is trapped with a dominant conspecific, appeasement seems to de-escalate the conflict and lower the cost of losing. Different mammals have different appeasement behaviors. A related phenomenon in which the subordinate and dominant develop social bonding is known variously as "capture bonding", "reverted escape", or the "Stockholm Syndrome". Dr. Joseph Carver provides this heuristic list of factors present in situations were the victim becomes emotionally attached to the abuser:

1. The presence of a perceived threat to one's physical or psychological survival and the belief that the abuser would carry out the threat.
2. The presence of a perceived small kindness from the abuser to the victim.
3. Isolation from perspectives other than those of the abuser.
4. The perceived inability to escape the situation.

The prevalence of dominance/subordinate concepts in animal training suggests that it has a pragmatic value. More research into appeasement behaviors of horses, and specifically the capacity for trans-species appeasement might make sense of the apparent discrepancy between the prediction of theory and the success of traditional and ethological based training paradigms.

Chapter 22.4

Trainer Consequences

Trouble shooting Training Problems.

> **The animal isn't naughty.**
> You made one or more of these mistakes.
> ☐ Not doing enough respondent conditioning;
> ☐ Rewarding more than one behavior in response to a cue;
> ☐ Reinforcing the wrong response;
> ☐ Reinforcing inconsistent responses;
> ☐ Not offering a consistent cue;
> ☐ Using too many cues;
> ☐ Not having a motivating reinforcer or having too much motivation;
> ☐ Not delivering the consequence with contiguity;
> ☐ Not consolidating a behavior before going to the next approximation;
> ☐ Not reading the animal's body language for problems;
> ☐ Not preventing accidental expressions of flight responses;
> ☐ Lumping too much behavior into an approximation;
> ☐ Not limiting random behaviors.

If I am not totally consistent and the animal needs a high level of predictability, the animal has to constantly keep alert for any indication that it might need to flee. If my animal is uncomfortable, the very first thing I need to do is become very predictable. In contrast, if my animal is so comfortable with me that boredom is setting in, I need to become relatively unpredictable.

Lack of motivation is a totally different problem than lack of understanding. Emotional arousal can look like lack of motivation. I approach it with respondent conditioning which could be pairing training with control and food through a simple well practiced operant behavior. Changing reinforcers can sometimes solve motivation problems, unless satiation has become the problem. Problems with communication should be addressed by breaking down the behavior to smaller approximations and by providing more information to the animal. These procedural adjustments get me through most kinds of problems.

There are some common problems with non-wild animals. Anticipation can be frustrating because it means that I trained the animal to do a bad thing. The net effect of anticipation in a relaxed animal is that the animal stops waiting for the cue and starts spending a lot of energy on guessing what the trainer wants. The way I avoid anticipation from developing is to keep varying the requests and making myself less predictable. But I never forego clarity of communication to make myself less predictable. I just ask them for a bigger repertoire and keep shuffling my requests into new combinations and sequences.

If the animal is trying to find the right behavior to earn reinforcement but foundering and I give the request more than once (because I have a hard time being strict), I then reduce the size the reward in my hand so there is a reinforcement for trying, but not a generous one. After I have asked three times, then I need to stop and reformulate a plan that will help the animal succeed. I look for a intermediate step or a similar task that will make a better learning set.

When I ask the animal for a behavior it is either going to respond by ignoring me, avoiding me, or trying to do what it thinks I want it to do. If I ask it for the behavior again while it is ignoring or leaving, I am giving it the opportunity to practice ignoring or leaving me. Not useful! Time to quit cueing and evaluate why the animal is not motivated to play the game. But if the animal is trying to find the answer, I provide him with more information and ask again. I consistently indicate incorrect actions with a gentle no-reward marker to signal that the game is still on and they should guess again. After three requests, I remind myself to stop and find a different way through the impasse. That part is hard! Then I either go back to the last successful criteria, or analyze why the animal is getting it wrong and do some remedial work.

I try to always come back to problem behaviors with a specific plan as to how to advance on the goal. In mustang season, there are usually enough interns here to make a very productive brainstorming session looking for solutions for individual problems (even if I already know what the best one is). A little doodling with contingency statements on the white board yields some fruitful approaches and it is usually obvious why the best one is just that. Just listing the alternatives and their pros and cons is a very good way to reflect on training processes.

Personal Development as an Animal Trainer

The empowered animal trainer knows there is always an improvement just waiting to be made. It's the process of identifying a problem and finding a solution to it that makes a person really develop as a trainer. The hardest part is just being honest about the problems.

A trainer is challenged to be in such control of his or her own behavior that the animal naturally behaves as desired. Anything that gets in the way of being able to control one's own behavior is going to get in the way training animals. Becoming a zen master might be easier (but much less fun)!

It takes a while for a new trainer to acquire the habits needed for good training. You can teach yourself, but you must have the will power to change and the brutal honesty to admit the problems. Don't be too critical of yourself for the first month. Then when you have some success under your belt, if you open yourself up to criticism, the feedback can really help you become aware of areas for improvement. Through the punishment of being aware of your failures, the negative reinforcement that comes of being open to criticism, and reveling in the positive reinforcement of training success, you can become a great animal trainer.

Chapter 23

Professionalism

"Mistakes are just an opportunity to start again with more information."
Steve Martin and Susan Friedman

The surest way to become a great trainer is to set goals for yourself every day, stay open to learning, look for chances to improve your methods, remind yourself not to be too predictable, and be strict about your criteria. The more animals you train, the better you are going to get, providing that you constantly look for ways to improve. So you just have to roll out of bed in the morning and be excited about getting to train animals that day. If you are very lucky, you will find a limitless source of animals and someone who will pay you to play with them.

According to the US Bureau of Labor in 2011, there are just under 10,000 animal trainers employed in the United States, making an average of $12 per hour. The highest paid animal trainers are in the entertainment industry and they typically make closer to $25 per hour. Training people to train animals usually pays better than actually training the animal. The bottom line to this paragraph is that you aren't going to get rich training animals; you have to do it because animal training is your addiction and it's very enabling to get paid for doing it.

If I was younger and just starting out my career, education and certification would be higher priorities for me personally. As time goes on, I think these things might become increasingly important, but the animal trainers working in the part of the country where I live are not academically educated. If I was trying to market myself as an animal trainer in this area, I'd only have to start showing up at public venues with well-trained trick animals. If I opened a training business to the general public and hung out up a wall full of credentials and therefore expected a professional level fee, it just wouldn't happen. I'd probably have a well-trained parakeet next to my desk and an empty wallet. If you don't wear the mandatory cowboy hat around here, no one believes you are an animal trainer.

As it is, I am in competition for the mustang training dollars with people with absolutely NO credentials other than they claim to have trained a mustang before. No quality control as to whether or not it turned out okay, just that they have done it before. My academic credentials are absolutely worthless in this world. The only benefit is that I can wear a white lab coat into the training pen and people quit treating me like an old hippy that can't afford to buy a cowboy hat.

But I've been on the other end of the equation lately and have been trying to hire trainers and assistant trainers. It doesn't seem to be a career choice that many people are interested in. My only success with finding help is to go to extremely focused international opportunity websites and risk hiring someone on the basis of their internet presence. The result of that is that I've hired three people that never showed up. Local advertising has invariably yielded entry level help that needed to bring their five horses and three dogs, rabbit and pair of cats. Yikes!! Actually by some miracle a young animal trainer showed up on my doorstep last year because her mother wanted to show her the mustang training place and I finally got to hire a person with some understanding of operant conditioning. It was a true miracle. I hired her little brother too and I want them back this year.

I do not expect any positive reinforcement for giving you my opinion about credentials. (A cowboy hat will get you more clients.) The best I can hope for is that the people that are selling credentials and education choose to ignore me. In a war between animal trainers, the first person to use punishment loses.

There is a very compelling reason to join professional associations. It's called insurance. If they can't help you with insurance, then at least they can give you a forum at which to present your research. There are barriers to joining many of the associations that are much higher than the entry requirements to most academic associations. I qualify for several (except for having friends in the associations), but there is not enough motivation to get me over the barrier.

I was a plant taxonomist for many years and worked on rare plant problems. We botanists do not have a union, so there are no certification requirements for botanical work. To do archaeological work, there are certification requirements. A botanist and archaeologist are working side by side on some project -- guess who is making the most money? To try to institute a law that requires certification for training animals (especially horses) in the United States would set off a total Sagebrush Rebellion. I am sorry to say that the change to mandatory certification ain't gonna happen in my lifetime.

That's enough of talking about the cultural environment in which animal trainers in the U.S. operate! Let's talk about something we can do something about.... Becoming great trainers!

The first step toward becoming the best trainer possible is to take responsibility for your animal's behavior - no more blaming the animal. It is a crummy trainer that blames the animal for not responding appropriately to the training methods the trainer employs. Labels will cloud your thinking. Calling your animal hormonal, phobic, dominant, abused, obstinate, etc. isn't going to help. Neither is telling the story of how life ruined the animal. All animals can be trained. Period. It merely requires a savvy animal trainer.

The second part of becoming a great trainer is to track your success by collecting data. Collect enough data and you'll have some great research to present at the association meetings.

Here is a list of the forms I keep and how I use them:

>**Animal Permanent Record**. I keep one form with the name of the animal, it's owner or previous owner, the year it was born, its size, color, markings, it's tag number if it is a mustang and a photo. I keep vaccination and worming history on this record. This report is generated from adding this information to our database when an

animal arrives. Our permanent animals also have their titles; while the animals in for training have their Coggins test reports and Care & Maintenance Agreements. The status of the animal (permanent resident, adoptable, adopted, boarding, private-training) can be updated in the database, and is used to populate the list of available horses for the adoption staff.

List of Goals for each animal. I keep a check list of tasks for each animal. Our training program is very criteria oriented. The mustangs have 26 tasks to master. We note when we start training each task. When we are done with the animal and it has gone to its new home, we file the goals with the permanent record sheet in the archives.

Data Collection sheets. For our wild horse gentling program, we collect records for every training session. The record specifies what the goal of the session was, and how comfortable the horse was at the start of the session and at the end of the session. The record has a space to record beginning and ending measurements of behavior. Each of our behaviors has a predefined type of measurement to record; many are frequencies and durations, but we also allow yes/no answers, percent successful attempts, and latencies. The type of measurement is defined by the behavior and the goal. The training record then has a space used to describe the intervention or training that happened between the beginning and ending measurements. We keep track of the session length in minutes and then give ourselves a subjective rating as to how good of a session it was.

What does it mean to set your animal up to succeed? The animal is showing it is ready, everything is in place, and you know what you are asking for. These things make a difference. What does it mean to set yourself up to succeed? You got it!

Made in the USA
Columbia, SC
29 May 2017